Wild in the City

Fauna & Flora of Colorado Urban Spaces

Heidi Snyder & Dorothy DePaulo

Westcliffe Publishers

BOULDER

Acknowledgments

Throughout the three years it took to put this book together we relied on the assistance of many generous friends, We would like to thank: Selma Payne, Denise Tomlin, Andy Kratz, Bruce Benninghoff, Mary Ann Bonnell, Chuck and Theresa Renstrom, Mira Perrizo, Kari Luraas, and all of our friends at RMSBA and ASBA. They offered their support, time, and expertise to help turn a mountain of photos, text, illustrations, and information into a cohesive, beautiful and accurate whole. We are so very grateful for what they have done.

This publication was made possible in part by a grant from the American Society of Botanical Artists.

Published by Johnson Books
a Big Earth Publishing company
3005 Center Green Drive, Suite 225
Boulder, Colorado 80301
800-258-5830
www.bigearthpublishing.com

Cover and text design by D.K. Luraas

9 8 7 6 5 4 3 2 1

Library of Congress Control Number: 2015944284
ISBN: 978-1-56579-666-9

Printed in Korea by Four Colour Print Group

Contents

Introduction

It all began with a walk in the park.

One spring day in 2011, my friend and fellow artist, Heidi Snyder, and I were walking in a Denver-area park. Although we had both walked there many times before, on this particular day we noticed a plant that neither of us had seen before, and we were determined to find out what it was. Then we saw another plant that was new to us, and then another.

It suddenly dawned on us that this park wasn't just a place where there are trees and grass and water with walking paths weaving among them. This park, like all parks, was made up of thousands—no, millions—of living things, most of which we knew very little about.

At that time, Heidi and I both considered ourselves primarily "botanical" artists. We both loved plants and liked to draw them. We thought it would be a "fun little project" to depict our local urban parks and open spaces by doing portraits of the plants that grew there, and so we set out on a quest to do just that.

Sometimes individually, and sometimes together, over the next three years we made daily trips to many Denver-metro area parks and open spaces. Almost every day we found plants that were new to us. As we found them, we did sketches and took photographs, and then we retired to our individual studios to work on our final drawings. We were learning so much, and we were having a wonderful time doing it!

As we looked closely at the individual plants, we also began to notice the animals that lived among those plants. There were birds and butterflies, reptiles and insects, and even fish and mammals!

"What kind of butterfly do you think that is?" "What kind of bird is that perched on the cattail?" It seemed only natural that we should attempt to do portraits of the animals as well as the plants. It was fun to draw plants, and we found that it was just as much fun to draw the animals!

We researched what we were seeing and drawing. What we learned made us marvel even more at the absolutely amazing wild environment right here within the borders of a very busy city. It made us love and respect nature even more.

We don't pretend to be botanists or zoologists, but we have done our best to depict each plant and animal that we've chosen as accurately as possible. We are far from done with our "fun little project," but we feel that it is time to share some of what we have discovered.

Although we have documented these plants and animals in our own local parks and open spaces, all of them without exception are found in other places. We hope you will look for these and others as well, wherever you might live or travel.

We would like to pass on to you the art and some of the knowledge that we have accumulated over the past few years so that you can gain from our experience. Hopefully we'll inspire you to take a closer look at your own little "urban oasis" wherever that may be, and find a new level of enjoyment at what you see.

Blue Spruce

Picea pungens

Heidi: I look around one morning in early May and the sky is an electric bright blue in contrast to the new-growth green of the trees and the red pine cones: a color feast for the eyes! But wait … the cones are red? And they stand up instead of hang down? What is going on? My little botanical universe was literally turned upside down and I began a search to find out what kind of tree I was looking at. After many hours of pouring over books and doing online research, I learned that I was dealing with a blue spruce, whose reddish cones stand upright early in the year, then drop later on and turn brown—who would have thought?

This is a large evergreen tree with blue-green foliage and a conical crown of stout, horizontal branches in rows. The needles spread on all sides of the twig from very short leaf stalks. They are four-angled, sharp-pointed and stiff, and have a pleasant odor when crushed. The blue tint of its foliage is caused by waxes on the needles' surface. The cones are two to four inches long, light brown, and cylindrical.

Blue spruce is a native species of the central and southern Rocky Mountains and a popular Christmas tree. Dozens of cultivated forms are available, bred for various shape and color characteristics such as red cone buds.

Colorado Blue Spruce
Picea pungens

Cattail Habitat

Typha latifolia

Heidi: I love cattails—almost as much as ducks. I love them! Wherever I go there they are, hiding my waterfowl, turtles, and frogs, providing nesting sites for birds and ducks and habitat for insects, as well as providing so many other uses for us humans.

In order to depict the cattail roots for this image (I had no clue what they looked like), I went out to my favorite pond and, while barefoot in the mud, tried yanking out the roots—easier said than done! And to think cattail roots were a staple in many Native American diets. I finally managed to drag a slimy sample home.

However, before I set pencil to paper, I had carefully constructed this image in order to provide as much information as possible. I highlighted the different stages of the cattail from flowering to seed by placing them in front of a dark background. This dark background also shows off the structure of the plant to its best advantage. The animals are placed according to species specification. For example, the yellowish dragonfly called "wandering glider" could only be placed upright, because that is what this type of dragonfly does. With so much invested in this piece, it was truly a labor of love.

Cattails are a common perennial with large creeping rhizomes (roots). The stems are simple, erect, and pithy. The leaves are long, linear, and flat. The mature "flower stalk" is velvety brown and eventually falls apart and releases tiny, tufted airborne fruit. They are usually found in wet or marshy places.

The tender parts of young shoots and green flower spikes have been cooked and used as food by Native Americans. Cattail pollen has been used to thicken sauces and mixed with flour for baking. The starchy white core of the rootstock was eaten raw, baked, or boiled and also ground into flour.

In the past, roots and leaves were used for caulking boats and barrels. Down from the flower spikes provided bedding, diapers, and baby powder. It was also used to stuff mattresses, pillows, and lifejackets and provided insulation and soundproofing. When mixed with ashes and lime, the down formed a cement as hard as marble. Cattail quilts are waterproof and therefore placed over mattresses. Leaves were woven into bed mats, chair seats, baskets, and water jugs. Cattail mats covered tipis and lodges. Cattail pollen was widely used in religious ceremonies, but later replaced with corn (Zea mays) pollen. Woven or bundled reeds served as floats and boats as far back as Sumerian times, approximately 5000 BCE, along the Euphrates and Tigris Rivers.

Wildlife: Dragonflies: red-tailed pennant, widow skimmer, yellowish wandering glider. Damselflies: mating bluets. Reptile: western painted turtle. Amphibian: woodhouse toad.

Common Goldeneye

Bucephala clangula

Dorothy: Before we started this project, I had no idea that so many ducks spent the winter here in the Denver area! I found the goldeneye ducks at several different lakes. They were new and unique to me and I wanted to capture them with my pencils!

For most of the winter, the common goldeneye can be seen in many Denver area lakes, but in the spring they return to their breeding grounds in the far north of Canada and Alaska.

Being diving birds, they may dive singly, but often flocks will dive together to capture aquatic invertebrates, and occasionally small fish and vegetation from the depths of the lake.

The male has a greenish-black head with a bright white oval on each side of his face at the base of his bill. His sides, breast and undersides are white and his outer wings and tail are black. He has a short triangular black bill. Like his name, his eyes are golden in color. The female's head is chocolate brown. Her outer wings and tail are brownish-gray while her flanks, belly, and breast are lighter gray. She has a short triangular bill. The color of the female's eye can vary from golden to white.

A female common goldeneye often lays eggs in the nest of another female, and she may lay in the nests of other species of ducks as well. Common goldeneyes and Barrow's goldeneyes lay in each other's nests, and wood ducks and hooded mergansers often lay in the goldeneye's nest, too.

After the ducklings leave the nest they can feed themselves and only require protection. Some females abandon their broods soon after hatching, and the young will join another female's brood. Such mixed broods are known as "crèches." They may also occur when a female loses some ducklings after a territorial fight with another female. Young scatter and mix when females fight, and not all of them get back to their mother when the fight ends. Some or all of the ducklings may be transferred to one brood, usually that of the territory owner.

At hatching, the eyes of a common goldeneye are gray-brown. They turn purple-blue, then blue, then green-blue as they age. By five months of age they have become clear pale green-yellow. The eyes will be bright yellow in adult males and pale yellow to white in females.

Both the breeding and winter habitat of these birds has been degraded by clearance and pollution.

Gadwall Couple

Anas strepera

Heidi: While I have seen gadwall ducks in many different settings, I was thunderstruck when I saw this softly hued pair swimming languidly in an iridescent pool of vibrant blue and liquid gold one sunny fall afternoon.

In a world where many ducks are brightly colored, the understated elegance of the gadwall is easy to overlook. The male sports subtle colors of gray, tan, and a soft, light reddish-brown. The female gadwall resembles the female mallard, except that her beak is darker and more narrow.

The gadwall is something of a pirate in that it snatches the food from diving ducks as they surface, thus getting food from places it can't reach. It feeds on aquatic plants and seeds, as well as a few insects and mollusks. In the fall, gadwalls often leave the water to forage for acorns. Pair bonding is established in winter and the gadwall returns to Colorado around May from the southern states or Mexico.

This is a fairly quiet species; the male has a hoarse whistling call and the female has a mallard-like quack.

Dragonflies

Black Saddlebag
Tramea lacerata

Heidi: Along the water's edge one can find these dragonfly wonders, which reveal their marvelous design upon closer inspection.

The saddlebag is a dragonfly genus that occurs in both the eastern and western hemispheres. Both sexes possess broad or narrow colored patches at the base of their hindwings—the "saddlebags" for which they are named. Some species are red, some black, with the females having duller coloring.

Saddlebags are familiar Southwest species, seen most frequently at lake edges and ponds. They spend much of their day in flight, but also perch on tips of tall weeds or shrubs in weedy fields.

Common Whitetail
Plathemis lydia

Two species of whitetails, so named because of the adult male's frosted bluish to white abdomen, are found in the Southwest. The whitetails have strongly patterned wings that aid in the identification of both sexes. This is especially useful before the males develop their distinctive, frosted appearance.

The common whitetail is widespread. It can be numerous at both moving and still water, where territorial males are involved in seemingly constant aerial chases. Both sexes perch close to the ground where they are easily seen. Females and young males are brown with pale streaks on the sides of the abdominal segments. Males of all ages have a small black patch at the base of the wings and a large black rectangle mid-wing. On females, the wing patch is a smaller one mid-wing and at the wing tip.

Lazuli Bunting

Passerina amoena

Dorothy: What a treat it was when I saw a pair of these little songbirds for the first time! Well, actually, it's been a treat every time I've spotted them. It's like finding a treasure! The coloring on the male is absolutely stunning. They have a unique-sounding song that makes them easier to spot if you follow the sound.

This beautifully colored songbird is common in shrubby areas throughout the American West. The male is easily recognized by its bright blue head and back, its conspicuous white wingbars, and its rusty breast and white belly. The female has a grayish brown head, nape, and back, with a bluish hint on the shoulders. There is a faint rust band on the chest blending to light brown on the belly. Her wing and tail feathers are brown with slightly blue-tinged edges.

Each male bunting two years of age or older sings only one song. Yearling males generally arrive on the breeding grounds without a song of their own. Shortly after arriving, it develops its own song, which can be a novel rearrangement of syllables, combinations of song fragments of several males, or a copy of the song of one particular older male.

The lazuli bunting has a unique pattern of molt and migration. Individuals begin their initial molt during late summer on the breeding grounds. Then they interrupt this molt and migrate to one of two known molting "hotspots." Some go to southern Arizona and New Mexico, and some go to the southern tip of Baja, California. At these locations, they finish molting. They then continue their migration to wintering grounds in western Mexico.

They live in bushy hillsides, wooded valleys, residential gardens, and in sagebrush along agricultural fields and hedges. They eat seeds, fruits, and insects, and are attracted to bird feeders.

Lazuli Bunting (female)
Passerina amoena

Eastern Cottonwood Tree (female)
Populus deltoides

Cottonwood Tree

Populus deltoides

Dorothy: As a child, I called a cottonwood tree in our neighborhood the "loving tree" because it had zillions of heart-shaped leaves. I did rubbings of the leaves to make valentines, not just on Valentine's Day, but all year round. The tree, to me, symbolized love.

Native to Colorado, the cottonwood tree is the largest and fastest growing tree in the state. It grows best in moist sandy soils next to streams.

Nearly everyone is familiar with the cotton-like fluff that fills the air in early summer. This is the cottonwood's way of dispersing its seeds. Not everyone knows, however, that this seed production happens only on the female trees.

Each cottonwood tree is either male or female, and the sex ratio is about one to one. Each tree sex has a flower, but the flowers are very different. Male flowers develop somewhat earlier than female buds and are much larger. They produce the pollen necessary to fertilize the female flowers. These flowers have forty to sixty stamens and are reddish in color and more conspicuous than the female flowers.

Female flowers elongate to six to twelve inches. They develop into the little pods containing the fluff that when ripe, burst open filling the air with "cotton" that floats to disperse the seeds. Trees as young as four or five years old have flowered. Seed production starts when the trees are five to ten years old, increasing rapidly in amount as the trees become older and larger. Estimates of annual seed production of a single mature tree have been as high as forty-eight million seeds, and good seed crops are the rule. A bushel of fresh fruit yields a little over two pounds of seeds, or about 770,000 cleaned seeds.

This "cotton" seed production that is considered a nuisance to many people may become a new source of bio-fuel. Because of its fast growth and yearly high yield of seeds, there has been considerable interest in cottonwood for energy fuels. There has also been interest in growing it for inclusion in cattle feed, since it is a good source of cellulose relatively free of undesirable components, such as tannins. The new growth is high in protein and minerals.

Lazuli Bunting
Passerina amoena

Cottonwood Tree
Populus deltoides

Black-headed Grosbeaks

Pheucticus melanocephalus

Heidi: I was ready to head home when I spied this black-headed grosbeak on the branch of a Douglas fir one July afternoon. When I composed the image I decided to add a monarch butterfly in the distance since the grosbeak is the only known creature that can safely consume the poisonous insect. Researchers theorize it might be due to the fact that both the bird and the butterfly overwinter in the same area in Mexico.

Black-headed grosbeaks (from the French *Gros bec* meaning "big beak"*)* are hefty songbirds of the finch family with very large bills, large heads, and short necks. Bill shape and size are indicative of a bird's diet and lifestyle. Here the mammoth bills of grosbeaks enable them to dine on a broad range of foods, from soft berries and insects to large, hard seeds. They feed readily on sunflower seeds at feeders.

Both sexes spend equal time sitting on eggs, feeding their young, and fiercely defending their territory. They can be found in open woodlands, thickets, and parks. The ideal habitat includes some large trees with a diverse understory, where caroling grosbeaks may be heard, but not seen.

Blackheaded grosbeak
euctius melanocephalus

Douglas fir
Pseudotsuga menziesii

Red-winged Blackbird

Agelaius phoeniceus

Dorothy: I'm not much of a winter person, so when I hear the beautiful song of the red-winged blackbird when it returns in early spring, I feel like I have been set free from the bleakness of winter. His song is truly music to me!

One of the most abundant birds across North America, the red-winged blackbird is a familiar sight atop cattails, along soggy roadsides, and on telephone wires. The glossy black males have scarlet and yellow shoulder patches that they can puff up or hide depending on how confident they feel. The females are a subdued streaky brown, looking almost like a large sparrow.

Male red-winged blackbirds fiercely defend their territories during the breeding season, spending more than a quarter of daylight hours in territory defense. He chases other males out of the territory and attacks nest predators, sometimes going after much larger animals, including horses and people.

In this species, males have many female mates—up to fifteen in some cases. In some populations, 90 percent of territorial males have more than one female nesting in their territories. But all is not as it seems: one-fourth to one-half of the nestlings turn out to have been sired by someone other than the territorial male.

These birds spend the breeding season in wet places like fresh or saltwater marshes and rice paddies, but they're also seen in drier places like sedge meadows, alfalfa fields, and fallow fields. Occasionally, red-winged blackbirds nest in wooded areas along waterways. In fall and winter, they congregate in agricultural fields, feedlots, pastures, and grassland.

In northern North America, red-winged blackbirds winter in the southern United States, as far as about 800 miles from their breeding ranges. Southern and some western populations don't migrate at all.

Fox Squirrel

Sciurus niger

Dorothy: I have a love-hate relationship with these little rodents. I marvel at their problem solving abilities and their persistence. I have yet to find a bird feeder that these cunning little animals have not found a way to invade. They are entertaining to watch, but they are also destructive. We have almost yearly problems with squirrels gnawing through the garage siding to get attic access for their winter nests.

The fox squirrel is one of three kinds of tree squirrels in Colorado. The other two are the Abert's squirrel and the American red squirrel. The fox squirrel is the largest tree squirrel in Colorado. The urban environment seems to make an ideal home for these little critters.

Their diet consists of tree buds, insects, tubers, bulbs, roots, bird eggs, pine nuts, fruit, and fungi. Agricultural crops such as corn, soybeans, oats, wheat, and fruit are also eaten.

Although they spend more time on the ground than other squirrels, fox squirrels are still agile climbers. They construct two types of homes. Their summer homes, called dreys, are often little more than platforms of sticks high in the branches of trees, while winter homes, called dens, are usually hollowed out areas in tree trunks.

Breeding pairs usually share these dens, but other than that, they are usually solitary and asocial creatures, coming together only in breeding season.

They have a large vocabulary, consisting most notably of an assortment of clucking and chucking sounds, and they send warnings of approaching threats with distress screams. They also make high-pitched whines during mating. When threatening another fox squirrel, they will stand upright and flick their tail over their back.

Bur Oak

Quercus macrocarpa

Dorothy: One early autumn day, I saw an oak tree that was covered in the biggest, weirdest acorns I had ever seen. I was familiar with the tree but had never seen an acorn on it, so this really piqued my curiosity. I picked one acorn and took lots of pictures of the tree and its many acorns with the fringe around their little caps. Then I went home to do some research. Two days later I went back to get a few more pictures and every acorn was gone—the squirrels had gotten every one!

The bur oak is native to North America, but is not a common tree in Colorado. It is a slow growing, large tree, in some areas growing to a height of one hundred feet at maturity, with a trunk diameter of thirty feet.

The tree is named for its acorn, which some say resembles the "bur" of a chestnut. It has the largest acorn of any oak tree, but produces acorns only every five or six years. The acorns are very large, about one to two inches long and one to one and a half inches broad, having a large cup that wraps much of the way around the nut, with large overlapping scales and a fringe at the edge of the cup.

In the evolutionary strategy known as masting, rather than producing seed crops each year, this tree produces large seed crops every few years. This apparently overwhelms the ability of seed predators to eat all the acorns, thus ensuring the survival of some seeds. These acorns are an important food source for small animals.

The leaves are three to six inches long and two to five inches broad, variable in shape, with a lobed margin. The flowers are greenish-yellow catkins, produced in the spring.

Quercus macrocarpa

Bur Oak

Common Mullein

Verbascum thapsus

Heidi: This noxious weed can be found just about anywhere, and as with all weeds (more or less vilified) I find a lot to be liked about this plant and tried to render it in that spirit.

This biennial produces a large, thick rosette of fuzzy leaves the first year, and a single, erect stout stem, two to six feet tall, the second year. The leaves are alternate and overlapping one another, light green, and densely woolly. The small yellow flowers around the stalk have five lobes. The fruits are two-chambered with numerous small brown seeds 1/32-inch long.

This noxious weed was introduced from Europe, but is a native of Asia and now common throughout temperate parts of North America. It grows along river bottoms, in pastures, meadows, fence rows, and waste areas.

The fuzzy leaves were smoked by Native Americans, used as padded insoles, or used in teas for treating chest colds, asthma, diarrhea, and kidney infections. They were also applied as poultices to ulcers, tumors, and hemorrhoids. Tea made from the stalk was used to treat cramps, fevers, and migraine headaches. Tea from the roots was taken to tone the bladder. Mullein-flower tea was said to have a sedative, painkilling effect. The stem and leaves also provided lamp wicks, and dried flower stalks dipped in tallow were burned as torches. Roman women used the flowers to make yellow hair dye, and soap made with mullein was said to return gray hair to its previous color.

Verbascum thapsus
Mullein

Heidrun

Prairie Coneflower

Ratibida columnifera

Heidi: I like to bring attention to often-overlooked minutiae, which are a hidden world unto themselves. The oblong blossom part of a prairie coneflower might only be an inch long, but enlarged it reveals the intricate design reminiscent of a pineapple.

Just having returned from a visit to my beloved Sonoran Desert, I wanted to show this simple, unassuming little blossom in front of a dramatic background reflecting the volcanic gray basalt rock of the desert. The "basalt" rim of the image forms the background for the sphinx moth, which occurs along the Front Range, but whose reference came from Tucson.

The prairie coneflower has yellow petals, the purple coneflower lavender ones, and the brown coneflower rusty-red ones. Flowers appear from July through September. The leaves are alternate, gray-green, and somewhat hairy.

The coneflower is an erect-growing perennial with its somewhat hairy stems, with the flower stem accounting for at least a third of its height. It grows in dry prairies, along roadsides or railway grades, and in open areas.

The painted image is surrounded by a border of white-lined sphinx moths (*Hyles lineata*). This moth is active by day and night, hovering like a hummingbird over a variety of flowers. There are two generations per year.

Mexican Hat   Ratibida columnifera

Heidrun

Curly Dock

Rumex crispus L.

Heidi: Here we go again—just another weed. I like weeds … they have a lot to teach us. Curly dock is usually shown with emphasis on the brown seed stage, but there is more to a plant than just its seeds.

This is a robust tap-rooted perennial growing two to five feet tall. The stems are erect, often reddish, and slightly ridged. The leaves are mostly basal with curly or wavy margins. The flower stalk and the entire plant turn reddish-brown at maturity.

All docks are said to be edible, and curly dock is one of the best. While even the young leaves are too sour to be eaten raw, they can provide an excellent cooked vegetable (often requiring changes of water). Docks often produce large quantities of fruit, which can be stripped from the plant and then winnowed to separate the outer hulls. These seeds can be boiled into mush or ground into flour for addition to breads, muffins, and gravies.

Curly dock leaves are rich in protein, calcium, iron, potassium, and vitamins. They can contain more vitamin C than oranges and more vitamin A than carrots. They are sometimes used as dusting power when dried, and powdered or applied as paste for healing sores and reducing itching. Root tea has been used to treat jaundice and some consider curly dock a liver stimulant. Dock plants contain a chemical compound called "anthraquinone," which has laxative and anti-bacterial effects and also stops the growth of ringworm and fungi.

Cassin's Finch and Skunkbush

Carpodacus cassinii

Heidi: With this image I wanted to show how well fauna and flora interact, more specifically how well the concept of camouflage works. The rather brightly colored finch almost disappears in the red foliage of the skunkbush.

This finch occurs in the mountains of western North America. The male of the species has an overall wash of crimson red that is especially bright on the crown, while the female is brown to gray with fine black streaks on her back and wings. Both have a heavily streaked white chest and belly. This is a small songbird with a peaked head, a short-medium tail and a straight bill. Look-alikes are the common house finch and purple finches.

While Cassin's finches live in evergreen forests in the mountains, they may move to lower elevations in the winter and do not migrate here in Colorado. This finch forages for seeds on the ground, but also eats evergreen buds, and willow and aspen catkins. It feeds heavily upon the seeds of pine and quaking aspen.

Skunkbush

Rhus trilobata

Also called three-leaved sumac, the fruits from skunkbush were eaten raw, boiled, or dried and then ground into meal by Native Americans. The berries and meal were often mixed with foods, especially sugar and corn. Skunkbush berries can be crushed, soaked in cold water, then strained to make a pink lemonade-like drink.

The leaves were chewed to cure stomachaches or were boiled to make a contraceptive tea. They were also used in poultices to relieve itching and mixed with tobacco and smoked. Leaves were boiled to produce a black dye for baskets, leather, and wool, and the ashes were used to set dyes.

Skunkbush branches were split lengthwise and woven into baskets and water bottles. Sun/shade hats were woven from smaller branches. Large stems were used to make bows or spear shafts.

Skunkbush abounds in the plains on dry rocky hillsides and numerous birds feed on the fruit, while the dense and low foliage of this shrub provides refuge.

The leaves have a very strong scent when crushed, hence its name.

Cassin's finch   Haemorhous cassinii

Rhus trilobata
Skunkbush sumac

Butterflies

Heidi: In a departure from my usual contextual renderings, I chose this traditional sampler style to depict these butterflies life-sized. About twenty other butterfly species wait to be depicted, but their minute size requires a more special approach. All the butterflies occur in the Denver-metro area and along the Front Range.

Monarch
Danaus plexippus

The adults occupy a wide variety of habitats. In late summer and early fall, many populations migrate southward to avoid frost; populations east of the Rockies fly to high-elevation fir forests in the mountain ranges of central Mexico; western populations migrate to patches of woodland dotting the Pacific Coast from Sonoma County south to Baja. Hibernating clusters of monarchs can be found hanging from eucalyptus trees in Pacific Grove, California. There are three to five generations per year, but commonly fewer than 10 percent of monarch eggs and caterpillars survive.

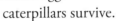

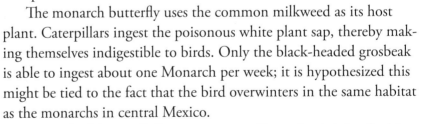

The monarch butterfly uses the common milkweed as its host plant. Caterpillars ingest the poisonous white plant sap, thereby making themselves indigestible to birds. Only the black-headed grosbeak is able to ingest about one Monarch per week; it is hypothesized this might be tied to the fact that the bird overwinters in the same habitat as the monarchs in central Mexico.

Sioux chief Sitting Bull, a proponent of homeland rights for his people, used the monarch as a symbol of always returning to one's homeland.

The monarch and its habitat are being considered for protection with the Endangered Species Act.

Monarch

Danaus plexippus

Two-tailed Swallowtail   *Papilio multicaudata*

Great Spangled Fritillary   Mourning Cloak

Speyeria Cybele   *Nymphalis antiopa*

Butterflies (continued)

Two-tailed Swallowtail
Papilio multicaudata

This butterfly has two tails on each hind wing. Adults fly in mountain habitats from late spring to fall. There is one generation per year in the Cascades and Rockies, with spring and fall generations in the Sierra Nevadas. The wings are darker and more yellow than those of the western tiger swallowtail.

Great Spangled Fritillary
Speyeria cybele

These butterflies fly in open habitats in prairies and woodlands. There is one generation per year. Western males are more orange than eastern varieties, darker toward the base, with black markings and spots. The female is much more tan rather than orange, with more dark at the wing base. The hind wings have large, silver spots.

Milbert's Tortoiseshell
Nymphalis milberti

The range of this butterfly stretches from Alaska to the Maritime Provinces and south to California and Mexico. It also occurs in the northern Great Plains, Great Lakes states, and New England, but is absent in most of southeastern and central United States.

The adults of this species occupy many open habitats, including moist woodlands, streambeds, rocky outcrops, and roads. There are two to three generations a year in the warm parts of their range.

The wings are distinctly two-toned above and below and have ragged margins. Above, the forewings have a dark brown base with two red-orange patches, a broad, pale outer band, and dark outer margins. Below, the wings have fine striations.

Douglas Fir

Pseudotsuga menziesii

Dorothy: I once stood next to a Douglas fir that was nearly a thousand years old. Although none of the trees are that old in the parks and open spaces in Denver, perhaps in the future they will attain that age. It makes me feel rather insignificant, but it makes me want to do my part in preserving these parks and open spaces.

Douglas firs are not a true fir, but are considered evergreens (trees that keep their needle-like leaves year round). There are two varieties of this species, coast Douglas fir and Rocky Mountain Douglas fir, which are differentiated by their habitats, growth rates, and physical characteristics.

When Douglas firs grow in dense forests, they self-prune their lower branches so that the conical crown starts many stories above the ground. Trees growing in open habitat, especially younger trees, have branches much closer to the ground.

Douglas firs can measure about 5 to 6 feet in diameter and grow up to up to 160 feet. The largest Douglas firs frequently exceed five hundred years of age and occasionally over a thousand years.

Douglas firs are conifers, meaning they produce seeds in cones rather than in flowers. The seeds have a single wing and are wind-dispersed. Douglas fir seeds provide food for a number of small mammals, including chipmunks, mice, shrews, and squirrels.

Douglas firs are one of the most valuable timber resources in the country. They're used for furniture, poles, fences, and flooring, just to name a few. Although they are harvested extensively for timber, Douglas firs are widespread and aren't in danger of extinction. However, when the trees are cut down, rare wildlife species like northern spotted owls may be threatened.

Rocky Mountain Douglas Fir Tree

Pseudotsuga menziesii

3 cm

Merlin Falcon

Falco columbarius

Heidi: Oh my gosh! Did I drive over something? I was getting ready to turn into a driveway on the edge of town one December morning when something fell straight out of the sky right in front of my car. I stopped, pulled over, and saw a bird with something in its beak flying up onto the roof of a house. Luckily it took its time to deal with its prey (from the looks probably a dark-headed junco), so I got quite a few good photographs before it took off. My first merlin, doing what it does best—dive-bombing its prey. Awesome!

This is a small compact falcon the size of a blue jay. Merlins are such swift and agile hunters due to their wings that are long and sharply tapered like those of jet fighters, allowing for diving maneuvers. Its nostrils are specially modified to allow it to breathe freely when flying at high speeds. Its four talons are large and sharp, forming a fearsome trap. Small birds are the mainstay of the merlin's diet, which it often catches in mid-flight, but it will also hunt large insects as well as small mammals.

Merlins are not very habitat-specific and can be found from sea level to treeline. In general, they prefer a mix of low- and medium-height vegetation with some trees.

Teasel

Dipsacus fullonum

Dorothy: The teasel is so difficult to draw! Every little spine has to come out at an exact angle. Some are foreshortened, and some are not. It took me a long time to complete this drawing mostly because I got so frustrated that I had to put it away. Much later, once I had forgotten how frustrating it was, I brought it out again and finished it.

The common teasel, although beautiful in dried plant arrangements, is an invasive species and in Colorado it is a "B List" species in the Colorado Noxious Weed Act. This means that the property owner must eliminate, contain, or suppress these plants from the property. Each plant can produce three thousand seeds annually so this is a difficult plant to deal with.

It is a biennial plant that occurs as a basal rosette until flower stems develop. The erect flower stems reach six feet in height and support spiny flower heads that are covered with small, lavender to white flowers from April to September.

Common teasel favors disturbed sites such as roadsides, ditches, wasteland, riparian sites, fields, and pastures. Only recently was common teasel distinguished from Fuller's teasel, which was once cultivated for the dried flower heads used in wool processing. Both are native to Europe.

Dipsacus fullonum

Teasel

Coyote

Canis latrans (barking dog)

Heidi: There he was, prowling the edge of the lake in a freezing late afternoon in winter, nose on the icy ground, circling back and forth to cover as much terrain as possible. Of course he knew I was there, sitting in the snow to reduce my profile, and finally he looked up, straight at me, to coolly assess me and the situation. He (or she) was beautiful: his fur was in excellent condition, he looked healthy and moved purposefully along on his route, no doubt in search of a nice (waterfowl?) dinner.

I saw him many more times that winter, always nose to the ground doing a perimeter check, and never scared or frightened, merely cautious and alert. That following spring and summer I encountered as many as five different juveniles, often in broad daylight, sometimes just a few feet away from me or other more oblivious passersby.

Historically the coyote was nocturnal, but now can often be seen during the day. It has adapted very well to urban life and its intelligence and knack for survival have long been its main characteristics. The coyote is formidable in the field with a keen sense of smell and vision. It is able to reach sprinting speeds of up to 40 mph and can jump up to heights of approximately four yards.

The coyote, about the size of a medium dog, lives in a burrow when not looking for food, and while it is more than capable of digging one itself, it often uses badger burrows, but will also use other hidden spots suitable to raising pups. Coyotes tend to associate as mated pairs and raise from three to twelve young in their den, which is the center of their territory. This territory may encompass up to twelve miles depending upon the availability of food.

Coyotes are omnivores and eat small rodents, insects, fruit, fish, carrion, waterfowl, birds, frogs, deer, snakes, and flowers. As opportunistic feeders they will also visit dumpsters.

They adapt their hunting styles and diet to their environment and in urban areas have been known to eat dog or cat food left outside, or even small dogs and cats. They may hunt alone or in packs, depending upon the size of the prey.

Coyotes vary greatly in color, much of it region-specific, and can reach a life span of around fourteen years in the wild. While their traditional enemies were wolves or bears, cars and traffic in urban areas now cause most fatalities.

While coyotes lack the many socially sophisticated facial expressions of wolves, they communicate through vocalization with a rather extensive vocabulary, including howling.

Over time coyotes have become well adapted to urban environments and in the process lost their fear of humans, which resulted in some negative/aggressive encounters. Currently the cities and counties of Denver, Aurora, Boulder, and Parker all have coyote management plans in place that have yielded positive results in that the number and severity of reported negative encounters between coyotes and humans have drastically decreased.

American Kestrel

Falco sparverius

Heidi: The "sparrow hawk" is North America's smallest falcon, approximately the size of a mourning dove. No other falcon has a rufous (rusty-red) back or tail. This is the only bird of prey where the male and the female have distinct colors: the male of the species has blue-gray wings, the female rufous ones. Both sexes have a black and white face with a double mustache. Similar to the kingfisher, this falcon hovers for prey on rapidly beating wings. The American kestrel may visit bird feeders and prey on smaller birds, but its preferred prey is small rodents and insects. It prefers high perches such as telephone poles or wires and hovers into the wind.

While it can be found in many different habitats, the kestrel prefers open country with short vegetation to better enable it to snatch prey from the ground. It nests in tree cavities, cliffs, buildings, and other structures. The American kestral is not long-lived, with a life-span of around five years for wild birds, while captives can live up to fifteen years. It stays year-round.

Falco sparverius
American Kestrel

Ambush Bug on Blanket Flower with Northern Crab Spider and Blanket Flower Moth

Heidi: It is amazing what one finds when one looks at the same old thing from a different angle!

Why, of all the times I had seen a blanket flower, did I pick this one to turn over and look at the blossom from underneath, and THEN take a picture? No rhyme or reason, but what exciting finds! I saw the moth, which blended in perfectly, and the ambush bug. I didn't even notice the translucent crab spider until I later examined my photos on the computer screen, and that's when the potential drama of prey and predator unfolded: ambush bugs feed on crab spiders. The crab spider feeds on insects such as bees. The blanket moth is completely dependent on the blanket flower and is potential prey for the ambush bug—wow! And all this drama beneath the petals of a small flower ...

Ambush bugs
(Phymata americana)

Ambush bugs are active during summer and fall in various open habitats such as gardens, meadows, and open roadsides. They perch by day on flowers, usually yellow blooms of plants in the aster family. They are "sit-and-wait" predators, attacking all kinds of insects that are often much larger than themselves. Adult males are smaller than females. Females lay eggs in froth-covered masses on plant stems.

Northern Crab Spider
(Misumenops asperatus)

This spider is active during the summer, occurring in open, grassy areas or habitats where there is low herbaceous growth or plenty of flowers. It ambushes insects that come to seek pollen and nectar.

Blanket Flower
(Gaillardia aristata)

This flower blooms July through August and grows along roadsides and drier uplands as far as the forest edge. It is an erect, upright, hairy-stemmed perennial growing from a slender tap-root, usually eight to twenty-four inches tall. The blanket flower comes in variations of yellow with a bit of red or the other way around, red with just a bit of yellow (the latter is referred to as the Indian blanket flower).

Blanket Flower Moth
(Schinia masoni)

This moth has burgundy forewings and a yellow head and thorax, which make it extremely well camouflaged when feeding or resting on the blossoms of the Indian blanket flower. This colorful moth is completely dependent on the native wildflower Indian blanket as its sole host plant. The female moth inserts eggs between the disk-flowers of the host plant. There the larvae hatch and eat the blanket flower seeds. Pupation takes place in the soil, and pupae probably wait one year before emerging as adults during the next blooming period of their host plant. *Schinia masoni* is generally rare.

Showy Milkweed with Monarch Butterfly

Heidi: Found in the vicinity of water, the showy milkweed displays its huge pink flower clusters that attract all kinds of pollinators, from the western tiger swallowtail, the monarch, and other butterflies, to bees and other insects. Decorative seedpods release their seeds on "parachutes" in late summer and fall, and throughout the year this common plant is uncommonly beautiful.

Showy Milkweed
Asclepias speciosa Torr.

Milkweeds can be divided into two, broad groups. The narrow-leaved milkweeds have linear or narrowly linear leaves. The second group is the broad-leaved milkweeds. Most of these have leaves that are at least 1.5 inches wide throughout much of their length.

Showy milkweed is a broad-leaved perennial, up to six feet tall, often occurring in large clumps. When stems and leaves are broken, a milky juice oozes out, hence the name. The blooms are numerous, pink to pinkish-purple, and form dense globular umbels that may be two to three inches across. The fruit is an elongated pod filled with numerous seeds, each having a tuft of long, silky hairs.

Although milkweeds are poisonous, they have been used as medicines for centuries. Flower buds and blossoms of several Great Plains species were used to thicken soup, roots were given to children with diarrhea, and tea from whole plants was said to be good for mothers to produce breast milk. Because of the generally toxic nature of milkweeds, such uses are *not* advised.

Monarch Butterfly
Danaus plexippus

Monarch butterflies lay their eggs on several milkweed species, making the milkweed the monarch's host plant. Developing larvae feed on the foliage, which in turn protects the larvae by making them distasteful and toxic to birds. The monarch is known throughout North America for its vast migrations and communal winter roostings (some in Pacific Grove, California, others in central Mexico), as well as its poisonous properties and resulting mimicry by the viceroy butterfly. The monarch's strong flight, averaging around ten miles per hour, enables them to evade predators relatively easily.

Asclepias speciosa
Common milkweed

Eastern Cottontail

Sylvilagus floridanus

Dorothy: One of my all-time favorite paintings is of a field hare done by German artist Albrecht Dürer in 1502. I did this colored pencil illustration as a tribute to Dürer. This is my version of that old painting. It is not a hare, however, but a cottontail rabbit.

The eastern cottontail is the most common species of rabbit in North America. They prefer open grassy areas, clearings, and fields supporting abundant green grasses and herbs, with shrubbery for cover. They are seldom found in deep woods.

Food items include bark, twigs, leaves, fruit, buds, flowers, grass seeds, sedge fruits, and rush seeds. Because eastern cottontails eat so many plants, they poop a lot. You can recognize it by the pile of dark-brown pea-size pellets. They actually have two different kinds of poop. One is a hard, brown pellet. The other is soft and green. Sometimes rabbits will eat very quickly and then go somewhere safe and undercover. They will drop these green pellets and eat them again later.

Eastern cottontails usually hop to get around, but they can run fast for short distances to avoid danger. They usually run in a zig-zag manner to break the scent trail. They can also leap up to fifteen feet.

The cottontail is prey for many animals including dogs, cats, coyotes, foxes, raccoons, great horned owls, hawks, snakes, and ravens.

Cottontails do not dig burrows. They nest in shallow depressions in grassy areas or in the abandoned burrows of other animals. The male may breed with several females and each female may have as many as thirty offspring a year.

Fritillary Butterflies on Yellow-spined Thistle

Cirsium scariosum, Nutt.

Heidi: The sun bakes the landscape in July and all the vegetation is a dull brown, having surrendered all color to the western sun. On the drab-looking meadow thistle, several variegated fritillary butterflies have gathered to collect the last bit of nectar before the thistle goes to seed. They provide an unexpected flash of color, turning this way and that, as their wings are highlighted by the brilliant sun.

I chose to depict this scene on a hand-colored gray background to really bring out the thistle's thorns and highlight the brilliant butterfly wings.

This thistle is an erect, tap-rooted perennial growing two to four feet tall. Stems and foliage are pale green, sometimes sparsely covered with a few side branches. The leaves are deeply toothed, with many narrow spine-tipped lobes. The flowers are creamy-white to pink and often appear to attach directly to the main stem.

The yellow-spined thistle is a native species and typically found in wet meadows, but also on dry slopes and banks. It usually blooms around June to July, offering its nectar to a host of butterflies, including the depicted variegated fritillaries (*Euptoieta claudia*). This butterfly species is equally at home in deserts and mountain meadows from spring to fall. Adult variegated fritillaries can tolerate light frost and are prone to great variation in size.

Fritillary spp. on Cirsium spp.

Heidrun

Barn Swallows

Hirundo rustica

Heidi: These little agile fliers are surprisingly common. I saw four to five juveniles late one summer all jostling for a perch on an old mullein stalk gone to seed. On numerous occasions I saw adults, in each case close by the water. I chose to focus on the juveniles because they still have the fluffiness of a fledgling, but the beginning of recognizable adult plumage.

The agile barn swallow nests all across Eurasia as well as much of North America. It darts gracefully over fields, barnyards, and open water in search of flying insect prey. The deeply forked tail sets it apart from all the other North American swallows. True to their name they build their cup-shaped nests almost exclusively on human-made structures.

When perched, the sparrow-sized barn swallow appears cone-shaped, with broad shoulders giving way to long tapered wings. The tail extends well beyond the wingtips and long outer feathers give the tail a forked appearance. Juvenile swallows are chubbier, with a shorter tail and gray-bluish backs, lacking the distinct cinnamon-colored underside and face of adult swallows.

Barn swallows feed on the wing, snagging insects from just above the ground or water up to one hundred feet in the air. They fly in bursts of straight flight and are capable of executing quick tight turns and straight dives.

Barn swallows can be found in open habitat from fields to parks, roadway edges, ponds, and meadows.

Barn Swallow
Hirundo rustica

Along the Shoreline

Heidi: Shorelines, pond edges, and small creeks teem with life and all manner of waterfowl, shorebirds, and other birds. What these birds all have in common is superb adaptation to their surroundings, be it long legs for wading, long beaks for probing the mud for food, or body coloration that helps them blend in with their environment.

Snowy Egret
Egretta thula

The snowy egret is brilliant white with black legs and bright yellow feet. These feet play a role in stirring up small aquatic animals as the egret feeds. According to researchers, foot-stirring requires an egret to swish one foot through the pond mire while keeping the other planted for balance. Because its feet gleam bright yellow, the sight of one flashing by often startles frogs and fish into motion. Once spied by the egret, they are promptly skewered on its long, pointy bill. Foot-stirring means that the snowy egret sticks its foot deep into the mud and moves it about with purposeful strokes.

Snowy egrets wade in shallow water to spear fish and other aquatic animals. While they may employ a sit and wait technique to capture food, they may also run back and forth through the water, chasing their prey with wings spread.

During the breeding season, the snowy egret grows curvy, filmy plumes that once fetched astronomical prices in the fashion industry, endangering the species.

Along the Shoreline (continued)

Greater Yellowlegs
Tringa melanoleuca

This is a long-legged shorebird of tidal marshes and freshwater ponds. Its long legs enable it to wade farther from shore, where it sweeps the water for invertebrates and small fish. The nest consists of a hollow in moss near water, where the female usually lays four eggs and tends to the hatchlings for about twenty days.

Spotted Sandpiper
Actitis macularia

This is one of many shore birds occurring across North America. Spotted sandpipers are handsome and also have distinct social lives in which females take the lead. They return first to the nesting site, fight with other females over territory, and often pair with several males, laying several clutches of eggs, and participating in parental duties only with their last partner, leaving the previous males to raise the young. During breeding season, sandpipers have bold spots on their chest and an orange bill; in the winter the chest is white and the bill is pale yellow. Spotted sandpipers are often solitary, walking with a distinct teeter while constantly bobbing their tails up and down.

Least Sandpiper
Calidris minutilla

This tiniest member of the sandpiper family is no larger than a sparrow and colored like the sands and surf of beaches and shorelines, with greenish-yellow legs and a short, slim bill. Breeding adults are brown above with rusty and buff feather edges. Their underparts are whitish with streaks on the breast.

It inhabits mud flats, marshes, and beaches, feeds mainly on crustaceans and insects, and nests on tundra. The nest is a small hole in the ground that is lined with grass or leaves. There are usually four eggs that are incubated for nineteen to twenty-three days, primarily by the male who also tends the hatchlings.

Killdeer
Charadrius vociferous

The killdeer is a plover common to golf courses, lawns, athletic fields, and parking lots, as well as mudflats and sandbars. This species is one of the least water-associated species of all shorebirds. This tawny bird runs across the ground in spurts, stopping with a jolt to see if they have startled up any insect prey. When disturbed they break into flight, circling overhead and calling "killdeer."

Young killdeer—sporting only one stripe—follow their parents within hours of birth and "freeze" at the slightest sign of danger while their parents fly in the face of the oncoming danger, trying to lead it away by pretending to be injured. But if the parents signal them to flee the chicks dash away, sometimes into a stream or pond where they swim away. If the predator is a hawk, they drop beneath the surface and swim safely underwater. Killdeer nests are a scrape in the ground, lined with bits of grass, pebbles, and stems.

Mallard

Anas platyrhynchos

Dorothy: When we first started this project, I spent an entire summer looking for a male mallard. I knew it was the male that had the beautiful green head, but I saw no green heads anywhere! It wasn't until later when I did some research that I found out the males shed their bright feathers after breeding season, so during the summer the males and females look pretty much alike.

Perhaps the most familiar of all ducks, mallards live throughout North America and Eurasia. The male's gleaming green head, gray flanks, and black tail curl make it one of the easiest ducks to identify. Almost all domestic ducks come from this species.

Mallards are "dabbling ducks," meaning they feed in the water by tipping forward and grazing on underwater plants. They almost never dive. They can be very tame ducks especially in city ponds. They often group together with other mallards or other species of dabbling ducks.

Mallard pairs are generally monogamous, but paired males pursue females other than their mates. Extra-pair copulations are common among birds and in many species are consensual, but male mallards often force these copulations, with several males chasing a single female and then mating with her.

The standard duck's quack is the sound of a female mallard. Males don't quack, they make a quieter, rasping sound.

Mallards, like other ducks, shed all their flight feathers at the end of the breeding season and are flightless for three to four weeks. They are secretive during this vulnerable time, and their body feathers molt into a concealing "eclipse" plumage that can make them hard to identify.

Western Painted Turtle

Chrysemis picta bellii

Heidi: When I saw my first mud-splattered little reptile/turtle, I was so happy I called my friend on the phone and squealed. That began my journey into the wild and reptilian world of the local painted turtle. Curiosity may kill the cat but it almost cost me a finger, when on June 20, 2013, I saw a BIG turtle quite a distance from the water. What was it doing there? Knowing that the pattern of its underside is as unique to it as a fingerprint is to us humans, I flipped it onto its back and took quick pictures. Upon flipping it back over I got down on all fours to get that awesome head to head shot, up close and personal. While I focused my camera I must have stuck out my pinky, because that obviously disgruntled turtle suddenly chomped down so hard that the blood ran and it hurt like heck. Luckily, it let go—some snapping turtles don't. So now I can truthfully state that I am the happy survivor of a reptile attack. And they say there is no excitement at the local pond …

The western painted turtle is named after the bright yellow stripes on its head, neck, legs, and tail and the glowing red on its plastron (shell covering the belly) and under-edge of its carapace (shell covering the back). Painted turtles have webbed hind feet and slender claws on their front feet. Males are smaller and have much longer claws than females. Painted turtles can grow to a foot in length.

The western painted turtle is the most northerly occurring turtle in America. It can survive in water at 20 degrees Fahrenheit and covered with two feet of ice.

Most turtles spend the winter hibernating in the mud at the bottom of ponds and lakes. Once the water warms and the ice melts, courtship begins with the male pursuing the female (but it can be the other way around). The mating takes place at the bottom of the pond. In June or July the female lays her eggs, which will not hatch until sometime in September. The hatchlings will stay in the nest until spring, but the survival rate is low due to freezing and predation.

To avoid predators (raccoons and skunks), turtles like to bask in the sun completely surrounded by water, often several turtles deep.

Painted turtles prefer the margins and shallows of lakes and ponds, ditches, and sluggish streams with muddy bottoms and lots of aquatic plants. They also require upland nesting areas without vegetation.

This reptile is an opportunistic omnivore, enjoying a wide variety of aquatic foods, such as insects, snails, worms, frogs, tadpoles, algae, aquatic plants, and carrion. All the food is swallowed underwater.

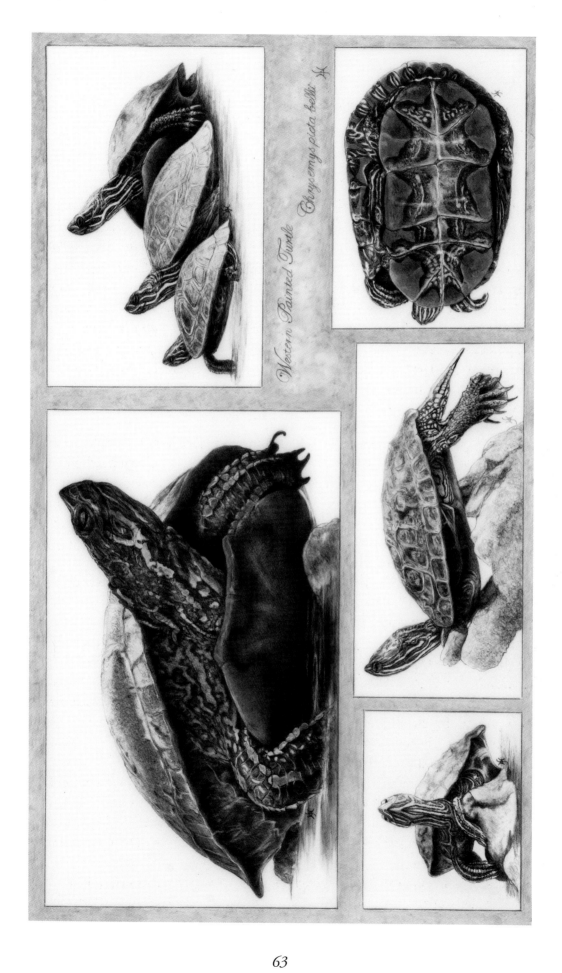

Canada Goose

Branta Canadensis

Dorothy: The honking "V" of a flock of Canada geese from overhead is a familiar winter sound. On the ground, I like their sassy attitude. The geese at a nearby park are so confident that they've taken to chasing my little dog! In my portrait of them I wanted to include both their attitude and also their flight pattern.

The Canada goose is the most common waterfowl in North America. Although some subspecies of this goose were hunted nearly to extinction in the early 1900s, today in many areas they have become so populous that they are considered pests. In urban areas there are fewer coyotes, fox, and bald eagles that all prey on geese, and food is prevalent.

These geese live in a great many habitats near water, grassy fields, and grain fields. They are particularly drawn to lawns for two reasons: they can digest grass and when they are feeding their young, manicured lawns give them a wide, unobstructed view of any approaching predators, which is why they're drawn to golf courses.

Some migratory populations of Canada geese are not going as far south in the winter as they used to. This northward range shift has been attributed to changes in farm practices that make waste grain more available, increasing availability of urban turf for grazing in fall and winter, as well as changes in hunting pressure and changes in weather.

At least eleven subspecies of the Canada goose have been recognized, although only a couple are distinctive. In general, the geese get smaller as you move northward, and darker as you go westward.

American Avocet

Recurvirostra Americana

Dorothy: Their beautiful coloring and the way they move so gracefully through the shallow waters is what inspired me to do a portrait of the American avocet. It was easy to spend hours watching how they move and react to one another.

In the late spring and throughout the summer, these birds can be found in the shallows of many lakes and other wetlands where they can be seen swinging their long upturned bills through the water to catch small invertebrates.

Their nests are usually just a scrape in the ground lined with grass. A female American avocet may lay one to four eggs in her own nest, or she might just as easily lay them in the nest of another female, who then incubates the eggs. American avocets have also been known to lay eggs in the nests of other kinds of birds, mew gulls for instance, and other species lay eggs in avocet nests. Avocets have incubated mixed clutches of their own eggs and those of common terns or black-necked stilts. The avocets rear the other hatchlings as if they were their own. The chicks leave the nest within twenty-four hours of hatching. Day-old avocets can walk, swim, and even dive to escape predators.

Bufflehead Pair

Bucephala albeola

Heidi: As a diving duck, buffleheads tend to hang out in the middle of a body of water where the water is the deepest. That, and the fact that they dive and you never know when and where they will resurface make them very difficult to photograph. "Buffy" and his girlfriend have elicited many colorful expletives on my part, and I used this reference photo because it was fairly sharp and I liked the fact that for once he didn't leave his girlfriend behind, but swam beside her.

The bufflehead is the smallest of the diving ducks. Its name comes from the shape of its head, which is large and prominent like that of a buffalo.

Buffleheads feed primarily on aquatic insects in the summer and snails and clams in the winter. They migrate from the boreal forest of Canada where each breeding pair claims a small lake on its arrival in spring, around March. The bufflehead's small body size is well adapted to nesting in tree cavities, usually those used by the northern flicker. Like female wood ducks, the bufflehead coaxes her young to leap to the ground where they will be led to a new territory where they learn to fly. Later in the summer they go with the female to join the males. Like other tree nesters, buffleheads have a strong homing instinct.

Belted Kingfisher

Megaceryle alcyon

Heidi: Since it was December and the trees were leafless, some movement up in the trees caught my attention—something blue. A blue jay perhaps? But it was the wrong season. Finally, I caught up to it with my camera. Flying from tree to tree along the water's edge, I recognized a female belted kingfisher.

The kingfisher patrols rivers and streams and feeds almost exclusively on aquatic prey, such as fish or crayfish for which its straight and heavy bill is well suited. It also flies up and down shorelines, giving loud rattling calls. It hunts by either plunging directly from its perch or by hovering over the water, bill pointed downward, ready to strike once it sees prey.

It nests in burrows along earthen banks, which it has hollowed out with its beak, removing debris with its feet. There it lays a clutch of eggs in total darkness. After about five weeks the chicks finally emerge from the chamber, and shortly thereafter fend for themselves.

The male of this species lacks the rusty chest belt that is found only on females. Migration depends on whether the kingfisher has access to open water, and thereby food.

Great Blue Heron

Ardea herodias

Dorothy: If I had to pick a favorite bird, it would probably be the great blue heron. I have spent more time watching them than any other bird. To me, they are absolutely fascinating! I've watched the adult herons build their nest. I've watched the hatchlings fight over food that their parents bring to the nest. I've seen a juvenile leave the nest for the first time. Two years ago, I watched a lone juvenile struggle to survive a bitter winter when all others had migrated south. (He did survive by the way!)

Whether poised at the edge of a pond or cruising a coastline, the great blue heron is a majestic sight. This stately heron with its subtle blue-gray plumage often stands motionless as it scans for prey or wades with long deliberate steps. They may move slowly, but they strike with lightning speed to grab a fish or snap up a frog.

Great blue herons have specialized feathers on their chest that continually grow and fray. The herons comb this "powder down" with a fringed claw on their middle toes, using the down like a washcloth to remove fish slime and other oils from their feathers as they preen. Applying the powder to their underparts protects their feathers against the slime and oils of swamps.

Great blue herons can hunt day and night thanks to a high percentage of rod-type photoreceptors in their eyes that improve their night vision. Despite their impressive size, they weigh only five to six pounds thanks in part to their hollow bones—a feature all birds share.

Pairs are mostly monogamous during a season, but they choose new partners each year. Away from the colony, great blue herons defend feeding territories from other herons with competitive displays in which the birds approach intruders with their head thrown back, wings outstretched, and bill pointing skyward. Gulls and humans may also be a target of this defensive maneuver.

Great Blue Heron (continued)

Double-crested Cormorant

Phalacrocorax auritus

Heidi: I was so proud, when years ago, I snapped this picture of a cormorant. Little did I know then that I had captured a lighter-colored juvenile … needless to say, my learning curve has been going uphill ever since, but "Cormie" will always be my first.

The double-crested cormorant got its name from the double crest of stringy black or white feathers above each eye that the adults develop during breeding season. While immature, the bird is chocolate brown with a light neck and chest that darkens to an overall matte-black as an adult. This is a large water bird with a heavy body and kinked neck that sits low in the water. It has yellow-orange facial skin and green eyes.

It nests high up in trees (usually in colonies) along lakes, harbors, or swamps, and any place where food (fish and crustaceans) is plentiful. The nest is made from sticks and odds and ends, and the young are fed regurgitated food.

Double-crested cormorants float low on the surface of the water and dive to catch fish. Its webbed feet, long neck, and hooked bill superbly equip it to catch its prey. It can achieve spectacular speeds on and under water, accelerating with tandem thrusts of large webbed feet and powerful wings. After diving they dry off by spreading their wings. They tend to fly in V-shaped flocks that shift and reform as birds alternate between bursts of choppy flapping and short glides.

Hooded Merganser

Lophodytes cucullatus

Heidi: Mergansers are so colorful and attractive that it is hard to ignore them. Out of all my references I chose one with a blue background to really set off the rust-tan body.

The hooded merganser is the smallest of North America's three merganser species. This duck is named for its prominent black-and-white crest, which is erect during courtship or when danger is detected. The female also has a crest, which is reddish brown in color. Unlike the striking male, the female has gray and brown plumage and brown eyes.

The hooded merganser's narrow bill is lined with serrations that help the duck prey on small fish, frogs, aquatic insects, and mollusks. Like wood ducks, hooded mergansers nest in tree cavities where they lay nine to eleven eggs, which take thirty to thirty-four days to hatch. The ducklings exit the nest by leaping to the ground, cushioned by their down.

Hooded mergansers breed in the north (southern Canada, Great Lakes states) and migrate south in the fall only when ice covers their feeding habitat. Most mergansers follow the Mississippi and Atlantic flyways and are not considered good table fare by duck hunters.

Northern Shoveler

Anas clypeata

Heidi: The northern shoveler is easily identified by its broad "spoon-like" bill, which has comb-like "teeth" along the upper and lower mandibles. These enable it to strain the pond for plant seeds, fingernail clams, beetles, and other creatures. Often two or more shovelers will form a rotating raft with their bodies, thus creating a whirlpool that draws food matter to the water surface where this dabbling duck can access it.

The male northern shoveler has a shiny green or dark blue head, white breast, and chestnut flanks and belly. The adult female has mottled brown plumage and a yellow bill. They prefer to nest in grassy areas away from open water. The drakes are very territorial during breeding season and will defend their territory and mate from competing males. Drakes also engage in elaborate courtship behaviors, both on the water and in the air.

This common and widespread duck winters in Colorado, but sometimes migrates to southern states, Mexico, or Central America. Despite their stout appearance, shovelers are nimble fliers.

Black-crowned Night Heron

Nycticorax nycticorax

Dorothy: I'll never forget the first time I saw this majestic bird. He swooped past me a few inches above my head and landed on a log in the pond next to me. Because it was dusk and he was so quiet in his flight, it sent prickles down my spine. I didn't stay spooked for long though. I watched him fish the pond until it was too dark to see.

The black-crowned night heron is the most common heron in North America. The adults are about 25 inches long, with a wingspan of about 45 inches. They have a short neck giving them a rather hunched appearance. They are medium blue-gray on the underparts with a black back, mantle, and crown. A white plume adorns the nape.

The face is light gray fading to white around their large red eyes. Their stout legs are yellow-green, but become pinkish at breeding time.

The juveniles, though smaller, have the same body type as the adults, but they have brown and gray speckled feathering.

These herons are most active at night when you may see their ghostly forms flying out from their daytime roosts to hunt for food. They feed on leeches, earthworms, insects, crayfish, clams, mussels, fish, amphibians, lizards, snakes, turtles, rodents, birds, and eggs. They also eat carrion and plant materials. Rather than stabbing their prey, they grasp it in their bills.

Black-crowned night herons normally feed between evening and early morning, avoiding competition with other heron species that use the same habitat during the day. They may feed during the day in the breeding season, however, when they need extra energy for nesting.

American White Pelican

Pelecanus erythrorhynchos

Dorothy: These huge birds are amazing to watch! They are so large and clumsy on land, yet when they are on the water and in the air, they have the grace of angels. Watching them fish and interact with one another is so entertaining. I just had to paint the pelican.

One of the largest birds in North America, the American white pelican is a majestic bird. In the air, they soar with incredible steadiness on broad black and white wings. With their large heads and huge bills, they have an almost prehistoric look. On the water they dip their pouched bill in the water to scoop up fish. They may tip up like a dabbling duck to get the fish, but they don't dive like the brown pelican. Sometimes for easy feeding, groups of pelicans work together to herd fish into shallow waters. They can be seen on lakes in the summer and near coastlines in the winter.

Apart from the difference in size, males and females look exactly alike. During the breeding season, both sexes grow a horny knob on top of the bill. The knob size depends on the individual's age and previous breeding experience and is shed after eggs are laid. Ornithologists believe that the function of this horny protuberance may be for protection. White pelicans compete for nesting sites by jabbing at each other with their beaks. The knob may act as a target and shield to protect their pouches.

American white pelicans and double-crested cormorants are often found together. They sometimes forage together (although they mainly hunt different fish and at different depths). Cormorants even nest individually or in groups within pelican colonies.

The American white pelican is protected by the Migratory Bird Act of 1918. Habitat loss is the largest known cause of nesting failure, with flooding and drought being recurring problems.

Muskrat

Ondatra zibethicus

Dorothy: I like to think of this little fellow as more like a "little beaver with a long tail," than a rat. They are quite shy and like to hide in the reeds, but I've seen them in many of our lakes and along rivers in the city.

Muskrats are semi-aquatic animals that live in practically all watery habitats, from cattail marshes and ponds to lakes and rivers. In Colorado they range from the edges of the alpine tundra through all other ecosystems in the riparian zone. At highest elevations they are largely restricted to beaver ponds. In agricultural areas they frequently use irrigation ditches for movement to more permanent water sources. They live in burrows in banks along the water source or in conical houses constructed of leafy vegetation.

Muskrats are primarily herbivorous but they will eat carrion, fish, crayfish, and mollusks, especially when plant materials are scarce or animal matter is readily available.

The body is stocky with a large, rounded head. The laterally flattened, scaly tail is about as long as the head and body. The hind feet are large and partially webbed, with stiff hairs fringing the toes. The forefeet are small and dexterous. The mouth can be closed behind the incisors, and the ears are valvular, meaning that they close when underwater. The eyes are relatively small and the ears are short, rounded, and barely visible above the surrounding fur. Most muskrats in Colorado have rich reddish-brown to blackish-brown fur with slightly paler underparts. The gray-brown under fur is very soft and overlain by longer, coarser guard hairs. The dense under fur is nearly impervious to water.

While swimming, muskrats and beavers are often misidentified for each other. In the water, the muskrat's long tail creates a wavy, back and forth windshield wiper-like pattern as it swims. The beaver's flat tail does not.

Wood Duck

Aix sponsa

Heidi: I spied the male sharing a small opening in the icy pond with dozens of other ducks one winter, and the female and young later the following summer. To unite this attractive family I surrounded them with a rim evoking wood grain, since trees are their home.

The wood duck is among one of the most beautiful of American waterfowl. Like their name implies, they live in wooded swamps, extensive cattail, small lakes, marshes, and streams, where they nest in tree cavities or nest boxes close to water. They are one of the few duck species equipped with strong claws so they can grip bark and perch on branches. Short broad wings and a broad tail help make them maneuverable when flying through woods.

The wood duck nests in tree cavities five to fifty feet above the ground. Eight to fourteen eggs hatch after twenty-eight to thirty-two days. Just a day after hatching, young wood ducks drop to the water and swim off with their mother. Wood ducks feed on aquatic plants, nuts, fruit, insects, small fish, and crustaceans.

Wood Duck

Aix sponsa

Ring-billed Gull

Larus delawarensis

Dorothy: Though often seen in the grocery parking lots or at the local landfill, I found these gulls napping in the sun in the shallows of a lake. Since they seem to have a reputation as a pest, I wanted to show them in a different light.

One of approximately fifteen species of gulls found in Colorado, the ring-billed gull is of medium size with a short slim yellow bill with a black ring around it. Adults are gray above with a white head, underparts, and tail, and they have yellow legs. During their first two years, however, they are mottled brown and gray with a pink bill and legs.

Ring-billed gulls often congregate around human activity at garbage dumps, parking lots, and freshly plowed fields, wherever they can find food. They are opportunistic feeders and are often seen feeding on garbage or whatever else they can find. They often soar in groups looking for food. This notably adaptable and bold feeder takes bread from children, soars to catch insects, and even plucks berries from trees.

In summer, they are common on costal beaches, but in winter they will often head inland, usually living near inland lakes and streams. Though they may fly many miles from their breeding sites, most ring-billed gulls return to the same breeding spot each year, often nesting only a few feet from where they were hatched. Many return to their same wintering spots as well. They nest in colonies on the ground, often on islands.

Because they were hunted for their plumage (used mostly in making ladies' hats) these birds almost reached extinction in the late 1800s. Recolonization occurred by the 1920s and the population exploded during the 1960s and '70s. Today the ring-billed gull may be the most populous gull in North America, with an estimated three to four million individuals (70 percent nesting in Canada).

Northern Leopard Frog and Water Lilies

Lithobates pipiens and Nymphaeaceae sp.

Dorothy: At a nearby lake there are water lilies whose ancestors were planted there seventy years ago, perhaps by someone visiting the park. Most water lilies grow only in temperate or tropical climates, but these particular lilies have adapted to survive many below zero winters and other harsh weather conditions. These groupings of lilies provide shelter and food for frogs that can often be found swimming or hopping among them. I wanted to show this little slice of water life.

Once the most abundant and widespread frog species in North America, massive declines of this species beginning in the 1970s has drastically reduced their number. Scientists have not determined the exact cause of this decline, but it is most likely a combination of pollution, water acidity, deforestation, and perhaps pesticides.

Northern leopard frogs are so named for the array of irregularly shaped dark spots that adorn their backs and legs. They are greenish-brown in color with a pearly white underside and light-colored ridges on either side of their backs. They are considered medium-size, reaching lengths of three to five inches (nose to rump). Females are slightly larger than males.

Their range is most of northern North America, except on the Pacific Coast. They generally live near ponds and marshes, but will often venture into well-covered grasslands as well, earning them their other common name, the meadow frog.

Their diet consists of insects, worms, smaller frogs, and even small birds and snakes. They sit still and wait for prey to happen by, then pounce with their powerful legs.

Leopard frogs were once widely collected not only for dissection but for the food industry (frog legs) as well.

Osprey

Pandion haliaetus

Heidi: I had seen ospreys slowly circling "riding the thermals" but nothing prepared me for seeing them up close. I was visiting my daughter when I detected nests high up in pine trees, perfect for perching and raising young out of harm's way. I followed the adults right through thickets and shrubs as they went on their hunting excursions to the water's edge. Here they displayed their true excellence: after having surveyed the water from a high perch, they soared high into the sky, then dove, feet first, talons spread, with increasing speed into the water and picked up fish, often two at a time. It was magnificent!

The osprey is the only raptor that plunges into the water feet first to catch fish. From heights of a hundred feet or more, it searches for fish swimming near the water surface, then folds its wings and dives headfirst like a missile. Refraction in the water distorts the picture, but the osprey takes this into account during the dive. Just before hitting the water the bird throws its taloned feet forward. It might emerge with one or two fish at the same time and carries the fish in a head-first position for better aerodynamics.

The osprey nest is very bulky and can be found up high on man-made towers or tall dead trees. An osprey pair will use the same nest season after season, adding material until the overburdened structure collapses. The osprey lays two to four eggs from which the young emerge thirty-two days later and then leave the nest eight weeks after that.

Looking skyward, the flying osprey is recognizable by its dark shoulder patches.

American Coot

Fulica americana

Dorothy: One of the things that fascinate me about coots is that they have the most unusual feet! Getting a good enough picture of the feet to use as a photo reference was a problem, however. If a coot is not swimming, they're walking through mud and other muck and it is hard to get a good look at the feet. I finally went to the Denver Museum of Nature and Science to see a stuffed specimen, where I could get a close-up look at all of their anatomical characteristics.

The American coot is one good reminder that not everything that floats is a duck. Their small head, scrawny legs, and weird feet reveal a different bird entirely! Although they often mix with ducks, they are more closely related to the sandhill crane than they are to a mallard or teal.

Although it swims like a duck, the American coot does not have webbed feet like a duck. Instead, each one of the coot's long toes has broad lobes of skin that help it kick through the water. The broad lobes fold back each time the bird lifts its foot so it doesn't impede walking on dry land, although it supports the bird's weight on mucky ground.

A slow and meticulous forager, the American coot plucks at plants while walking or swimming, dabbling with its head just underwater or in full dives. In flight, coots are clumsy and labored. To get airborne, they typically have to beat their wings while running across the water for many yards. Coots sometime gather in winter flocks of several thousand, often mixing with other waterfowl. They are known to steal food from others, including ducks. Coots may lay their eggs in the nests of other coots as well as Franklin's gulls, cinnamon teals, and redhead ducks.

Their nest material is woven into a shallow basket with a hollowed interior lined with finer smooth material to hold the eggs. The entire nest is generally a floating structure anchored to upright stalks.

Coots aren't hunted nearly as much as ducks since many hunters consider them inedible.

Ring-necked Duck

Aythya collaris

Heidi: I had good pictures of this duck. In order to emphasize its unique peaked head I chose a very simple background.

The male ring-necked duck is a sharply marked bird of gleaming black, gray, and white, and its bill is crossed by a white ring. The female of the species is a rich brown. A distinctive peaked head makes it easy to identify. Of all the diving ducks, it is the most likely to frequent shallow wetlands during migration where it feeds upon seeds, aquatic plants, insects, snails, and crustaceans. It normally winters in South America, but can be found in local ponds in Colorado during that time.

A pair of ring-necked ducks stay together only for reproduction, then separate. The female lays one egg per day until eight to ten eggs are laid. They are incubated twenty-five to twenty-nine days and the female may remain with the young until they are able to fly.

Ring-necked duck
Aythya collaris

House Sparrow

Passer domesticus

Heidi: At first blush this image may be a drab winter scene, but the sun has melted part of the ice. Between the water's reflection and those from the ice and the grassy edges, all colors of the rainbow appear, forming a beautiful, kaleidoscopic winter scene. Feel free to step in and lose yourself in quiet contemplation and discover the unexpected—a perfectly camouflaged house sparrow.

Preferring to nest close to man (*domesticus* is Latin for "belonging to a household"), the sparrow is a friendly bird. When the house sparrow was originally imported by Nicolas Pike from England in the 1850s, no one could have predicted that the newcomer would displace native bluebirds, tree swallows, and other cavity-nesting birds.

The house sparrow is a very social bird. They roost communally, their nests are usually grouped together in clumps, and they engage in social activities such as dust and water bathing and "social singing," where birds call together while congregated in bushes.

The house sparrow can now be found year-round at suburban feeders as well as cities and farms all over the United States and it flourishes in man-made and man-manipulated environments.

Black-capped Chickadee

Poecile atricapillus

Dorothy: These little birds are my favorite songbirds. I can't look at these little guys without smiling. Even in the cold of winter they seem cheerful. They are what I'm thinking about when I fill my bird feeder. It was a joy to do a portrait of them!

Chickadees may be found in any habitat that has trees or woody shrubs, from forests and wood lots to residential neighborhoods and parks, and sometimes weedy fields and cattail marshes. They frequently nest in birch or alder trees.

The black-capped chickadee hides seeds and other food items to eat later. Each item is placed in a different spot and the chickadee can remember thousands of hiding places.

Chickadee calls are complex and language-like, communicating information on identity and recognition of other flocks as well as predator alarms and contact calls. The more "dee" notes in a "chickadee-dee-dee" call, the higher the threat level.

Chickadees are active, acrobatic, curious, social birds that live in flocks, often associating with woodpeckers, nuthatches, warblers, vireos, and other small woodland species. They feed on insects and seeds, but seldom perch within several feet of one another while taking food or eating.

They can be found along the Front Range all year long.

Hermit Thrush

Catharus guttatus

Heidi: Right before a thunderstorm on a summer afternoon, with skies an ominous gray, I saw a movement on a very low cottonwood sapling and just aimed my camera, not knowing what it would yield. Much to my surprise, hidden in the foliage was this small juvenile hermit thrush—a lucky find.

The hermit thrush has a rich brown upper body, smudgy spots on the breast, and a reddish tail that sets it apart from similar species in its genus.

This shy bird hops and scrapes in leaf litter while foraging. It perches low to the ground on fallen logs and shrubs and often wanders into open areas such as forest clearings or trails. It can be found in conifer or mixed woods, forest floors, thickets, and parks.

The hermit thrush's song is ethereal and flute-like, consisting of a beginning note then several descending musical phrases in a minor key, repeated at different pitches.

It feeds on insects, spiders, earthworms, and fruit for which it often digs through leaf litter to find. Sometimes it will cock its tail and bob it slowly, while flicking its wings.

While the hermit thrush is a frequent winter companion in much of the country, it migrates to southern states from parts of Colorado.

American Bush Cranberry

Viburnum trilobum

Heidi: These tall bushes are hard to miss with their showy white flower clusters in spring and their bright red berries in late summer.

Also called *Viburnum opulus var. americanum* this is a big, spreading shrub that may grow fifteen feet tall and twelve feet wide. It has large, maple-like leaves that have three sharply toothed lobes and turns red in the fall. The inflorescence consists of a flat-topped flower cluster—an outer ring of large, white-petaled sterile flowers that surround tiny petal-less blos-

soms. The central cluster of tiny flowers produces round, red berries late in summer. This plant grows in the moist soil of foothill and montane forests.

Historically, Native Americans ate the acidic, tart bush-cranberries whenever available, be that raw, dried, boiled, or mixed with grease for winter use. The berries are an excellent winter survival food because they remain on the branches all winter and are much sweeter after freezing. Today they are usually boiled, strained, and used in jams and jellies, but require additional pectin.

The bark is said to have a sedative effect and has been widely used to relieve cramps, sore muscles, asthma, and convulsions. The vitamin C-rich berries also give a reddish-pink dye and the plant is used as a garden ornamental.

Viburnum trilobum

White-breasted Nuthatch

Sitta carolinensis

Heidi: I was really trying to focus on another bird altogether when this little guy hopped down a branch (yes, down) and I caught him in the act of having a late breakfast one June morning.

These little birds dart about, right side up on top of a limb or upside down on the bottom, sometimes scampering down the tree trunk headfirst. White-breasted nuthatches seem to defy gravity, but the stubby legs of these chunky birds are placed such that they are always in absolute balance, no matter what their position. Their toes are unusually long and so are their down-turned claws. The tiny hooks at the tips catch easily into the slightest roughness, allowing the birds to run back and forth and up and down as they search for insects, insect eggs, and larvae nestled in the bark.

Although nuthatches and woodpeckers share the role of gleaning insects from the trunks and larger limbs of trees, their different styles permit a division of the food source. Woodpeckers, braced back on their tails, hop *up* the tree, while nuthatches move *downward*, spotting whatever beetles or insects might have been missed by the woodpecker. True to its name, the nuthatch enjoys nuts and can be seen in winter foraging for acorns, hickory nuts, and other seeds.

Buckeye Tree

Aesculus glabra

Dorothy: In the park that is close to where I live, there is a tree that I walked by almost every day for years without notice. Then one spring day, just after we had started this project, I walked by and was truly amazed that it seemed to be decorated like a Christmas tree with hundreds of clusters of creamy white flowers. It was absolutely beautiful. I don't know how I missed the uniqueness of this tree all those years, but I felt like I'd suddenly found a treasure and I had to celebrate by doing a portrait of this buckeye tree!

This tree is native to North America but not to Colorado. It is a medium-sized deciduous tree that grows as tall as fifty feet. They are not planted as plentifully as many of our more common trees, but they seem to do well here.

Tall and sturdy, the buckeye is a member of the horse chestnut family. The fruit of the tree is a round or oblong spiny capsule about one and a half to two inches in diameter, containing one to three nut-like seeds that are brown with a whitish basal scar. The seeds are poisonous to humans in the raw state, but Native Americans cracked the nuts open and then pounded the seeds into flour. Apparently pounding and cooking this meal removed the poisonous toxins.

They also cut the seeds into pieces and mixed them with water for suppositories for hemorrhoids. The cut bark from the base of the tree was made into a poultice, which was placed on snakebites. Young buckeye shoots were sometimes used as spindles or twirling sticks in fire-making kits. Some tribes mashed buckeye nuts and poured the contents into quiet pools to stupefy or kill fish.

To this day, some people believe that it is good luck to carry a buckeye seed in their pocket.

3 cm

Aesculus glabra

Buckeye Tree

4 cm

Spotted Towhee

Pipilo maculates

Dorothy: I first spotted this little bird scraping for seeds under a bird feeder. I had never seen one before and I didn't know what it was. My first thought was that it was a "robin gone bad"! After bringing out the bird identification book, however, I was finally able to give this bird its correct name—the spotted towhee.

The spotted towhee is a large colorful sparrow residing in the West. When you catch sight of one, they're gleaming black above (females are grayish), spotted and striped with brilliant white. Their flanks match the dry leaves they spend much of their time hopping around in. They have red eyes. They can be hard to see but not hard to hear in the leaf litter.

They hop over the ground beneath dense tangles of shrubs scratching in leaf litter for food. They also climb into lower branches to search for insects and fruits, or to deliver their quick, buzzy song. Towhees can fly long distances, but more often make short, slow flights between patches of cover.

Early in the breeding season, male spotted towhees spend their mornings singing their hearts out trying to attract a mate. They have been recorded spending 70 to 90 percent of their mornings singing. Almost as soon as they attract a mate their attention shifts to other things, and they spend only about 5 percent of their time singing.

The spotted towhee and the very similar eastern towhee used to be considered the same species—the rufous-sided towhee. The two forms still occur together in the Great Plains, where they sometimes interbreed. This is a common evolutionary pattern in North American birds—a holdover from when the great ice sheets split the continent down the middle, isolating birds into eastern and western populations that eventually became new species.

European Buckthorn

Rhamnus cathartica

Heidi: While photographing a flower one summer, a branch with blackish-blue berries got in my way and literally in my face. Curious, I searched my reference books to see what it was. Since leaf shape and color and the berries were not enough for positive identification, I went back to the same plant the following spring to document its flowers as an additional clue. Finally, I not only had a positive identification, but had also learned that this particular type of plant had a very similar looking "cousin" growing in close proximity. No wonder I was confused!

This is a small tree or a large, thicket-forming shrub with deciduous, simple leaves. European buckthorn has curly peeling bark and the twigs often end in sharp thorns, hence the name. The leaves are glossy on top with three to five deep parallel veins on each side. The fruit is a glossy black, wide berry-like drupe, each on its own stalk, and usually has four seeds inside. It ripens late summer to fall and often stays on the shrub through the following spring.

European buckthorn was introduced to North America from Europe and Asia, naturalized in dry, open woods, and is considered invasive. It can be found along fencerows and roadsides. Native buckthorn species have alternate instead of opposite leaves and have been used as a strong purgative and laxative. The fruits are considered inedible due to their strong taste.

Rhamnus cathartica

European Buckthorn

Tricolored Orange-belted Bumblebee on Sunflower

Bombus ternarius on Helianthus annuus

Heidi: The ubiquitous common sunflower can grow up to eight feet tall and has hairy stems, large leaves, and flower heads up to five inches across. These heads follow the sun each day, facing eastward in the morning, and westward at sunset. When intermixed with other annuals, sunflowers provide a good cover for many species of wildlife. The seeds are enjoyed by birds, but are also used in breads, cereals, salads, and for oil production. The plant has been cultivated in Central and North America since pre-Columbian times.

Yellow dye from the flowers and black dye from the seeds were once important in Native American basketry and weaving. They also ground the seeds for flour and used the oil for cooking and dressing hair. Tea from the flowers was used for lung ailments and high fever, and poultices from the flowers were used for burns.

The tricolored orange-belted bumblebee is a ground-nesting social insect whose colony cycle lasts only one season and which is common throughout the northern parts of the United States and parts of Canada. They have a complex social structure with a reproductive queen caste and a multitude of sister workers. Tasks such as foraging, nursing, and nest maintenance are divided among the subordinates. Tricolored bumblebees are considered superior pollinators because they will collect pollen even in cold weather, which is also why they can be found at higher elevations than bees.

Bombus ternarius, like most members of its genus, is seasonal, which means the queen comes out of hibernation in late April to start a new colony. The bumblebee workers fly from May to October when the entire colony (except the hibernating queens) dies.

The queen and the workers have black heads with a few pale yellow hairs. Parts of the chest and abdominal segments are yellow, two or three abdominal segments are orange, the end segments are black. The queen and the workers are close in resemblance, but the queen is bigger. The male bumblebees, called drones, have a yellow head with a few black hairs. The coloration of their chest and abdomen is similar to that of the females, with the exception that the last abdominal segments are yellow and not black.

In the Meadow

Heidi: I love meadows—wild, weedy, grassy patches that never get mowed and have both desirable and undesirable (invasive) species in them, which are often overlooked or trampled on, but no less worthy of inspection and admiration.

The butterflies all belong to the family Pieridae and are the black-dotted cabbage white, the greenish orange sulphur, the yellowish clouded sulphur, and the little yellow.

White-stemmed evening Primrose
Oenothera nuttallii

This evening primrose is a perennial forb one to two feet tall with smooth, whitish bark. The flowers have four white petals about one inch long, fading to pink. They bloom in July and August and have a disagreeable odor. The leaf blades are pale green, narrow, one to two inches long, with or without stalks. This primrose favors dry, sandy rangelands, open woodlands, road edges, and margins of fields.

It is named for Thomas Nuttall, a naturalist who collected plants in a journey up the Mississippi River in 1811.

Smooth Beardtongue
Penstemon glaber

This blue penstemon is the most massive of the penstemon, capable of producing multiple stems, eight to twenty-four inches long. The leaves are opposite, glossy, smooth, and waxy. This June- and July-flowering perennial produces multiple blue to purple to violet blossoms that are densely clustered and often oriented to one side of the stem.

Smooth beardtongue is often found in disturbed areas such as road cuts and eroded banks.

It is worthless for grazing livestock, but deer may browse on it. Some Native Americans made a wet pack dressing for snakebite from the leaves. Leaf tea was used to stop vomiting. Smooth beardtongue is also used ornamentally.

In the Meadow (continued)

Dalmation Toadflax
Scrophulariaceae

This is a perennial up to three feet tall that reproduces by seed and underground rootstalks. The leaves are dense and alternate and the upper leaves are broad-based. The flowers grow in the upper part of the tall stalk and are two-lipped, three-quarters to one and a half inches long with a long spur, and yellow with an orange bearded throat. The fruit is a two-celled capsule with many irregularly angled seeds.

Dalmatian toadflax was introduced from southeastern Europe, probably as an ornamental. It is aggressive and can be found along roadsides and rangelands where it may crowd out desirable forage. With an extensive root system, waxy leaves, and two different ways to reproduce make toadflax difficult to manage. It is classified as a noxious weed.

Western Meadowlark

Sturnella neglecta

Heidi: It is March and blustery and cold, but what do I hear (and then see)? A meadowlark! Spring must be here at last! The bird perches on some pine needles on the ground, true to its nature as a bird of the prairie.

The western meadowlark is a bird of the open grasslands where it feeds on seeds and insects. It nests in shallow depressions at the roots of grassy clumps, weaving the tops of the blades together to make a dome above the nest. The male of the species tends to be polygynous (mating with several females), sometimes maintaining several nests in the same territory. The young leave the nest about twelve days after hatching, and there are usually two broods a year.

Meadowlarks are more easily seen than heard, unless you spot a male singing from a fence post. Look for western meadowlarks foraging on the ground alone or in loose flocks in the winter. When flushed, they fly low, gliding and flapping with short, stiff wing beats. They are known for their rich and lovely voices.

Norway Maple

Acer platanoides

Heidi: This drawing is a typical example of gathering references from many different locations at different times of the year in order to achieve an informative and appealing composition.

This is a small to medium-sized deciduous tree with a straight trunk and a dense rounded to oblong crown that produces deep shade (which is why it is often planted along sidewalks in new neighborhoods). The Norway maple is often confused with the sugar maple, but the Norway maple has larger, paired samaras (fruits with wing-like expansions), the leafstalk oozes with milk sap, and the bark is darker with narrower fissures.

Under ideal conditions in its native range, these trees may live up to 250 years, but in North America it often has a much shorter life expectancy, sometimes only sixty years. Especially when used along streets, it can have insufficient space for its root network. Norway maples are considered invasive.

Acer platanoides

Bullock's Oriole

Icterus bullockii

Dorothy: A friend of mine emailed me a picture of a Bullock's oriole that he had taken at his bird feeder. He lives only a few miles from me and I was feeling a little jealous that he had seen the little bird and I had not. Just two days later, however, while at a park I spied a pair that seemed to be there just to "pose" for me. So now I had my own pictures and I just had to draw these stunning little birds. Although I had pictures of them sitting on a fence, I chose to put them on a flowering oak branch that I had seen that same day.

This beautiful songbird is a real treat to see in the wild. On the male, notice the black eyeline and black on his chin and center of his throat. His middle tail feather is black and the rest are yellow. His wing feathers are black and edged in white with a white patch on his wing.

The female is yellowish-gray on the underparts, which becomes paler on the belly. Her wings are gray-brown with one or two distinct wing bars.

The juvenile males resemble the adult female but are generally yellower on the underparts, and usually have some black feathers. Juvenile females look like adult females.

Both sexes of Bullock's oriole sing, but the males and females sing slightly different songs. The song of the female is similar to that of the male, but with harsher notes and a different ending. Early in the nesting period, and before and during nest building, the female sings regularly, and may sing more than the male. They like to nest in trees along rivers or in tall trees in wood lots and parks, and are especially fond of cottonwoods.

They mainly eat insects, berries, and nectar. In some locations, they may be seen using hummingbird feeders. They fly south to Mexico in winter.

At one time, this species and the Baltimore oriole were considered to be a single species, called the northern oriole.

Chokecherry

Prunus Virginiana

Dorothy: A fond childhood memory that I have is of my brother and I picking chokecherries along a country road and taking them home to my mother who made the most delicious jelly from them. While doing the painting of the chokecherries, I could almost taste that sweet-tart flavor!

The chokecherry is a shrub or small tree growing to a maximum of about twelve feet in height. It is native to North America and is found in most of the United States except in the very South. They are found in many parks and open spaces in the Front Range area.

Chokecherry leaves are oval, about one and a quarter to three inches long, with a coarsely serrated margin. The flowers are produced in clusters in late spring (well after leaf emergence). The fruit are about a quarter of an inch in diameter, ranging in color from bright red to black, with a very astringent taste, being both somewhat sour and somewhat bitter. The very ripe berries are dark in color and are less astringent and sweeter than the red berries.

The berries are an important food source for many species of birds as well as bears, coyotes, and foxes, so don't eat them! Leave them for wildlife. Native food collection for human consumption denies wild animals essential winter fattening resources. That doesn't mean we can't have them. They are cultivated in some areas and are used to make jellies, syrups, and wine that we can enjoy.

Chokecherry

Prunus virginiana

3 cm

DD

Northern Flicker

Colaptes auratus

Heidi: They are everywhere, those flickers—in the park, on your house, in your backyard, on the ground, and in the air. They peck at ants on the ground as eagerly as on your house roof and consequently are not always welcome. But seen in the wild on a sunny winter morning, hanging from a hole in a big old cottonwood tree, I admired how well they have adapted to their surroundings.

The northern flicker is a type of woodpecker that spends a great deal of time on the ground searching for fallen fruits, seeds—and above all ants, of which it consumes more than any other North American bird. It has a tongue that extends nearly three inches beyond its beak and is ideally suited for this purpose. They can also be seen perching vertically on branches or tree trunks (instead of leaning against their tails). The flicker uses trees for nesting, but has also adapted to farmlands, parks, poles, and even houses.

Its appearance differs from region to region and has great variation, with the male more colorful than the female, which lacks the male's characteristic mustache. When they fly you see a flash of color in the wings—yellow in the East, orangeish-red in the West, and a bright white flash on the rump. They fly in an up and down path with heavy wing flaps interspersed with glides, like many woodpeckers.

Smooth Sumac

Rhus glabra

Heidi: The omnipresent sumac is too attractive with its red seeds and bright colorful fall leaves to be passed up.

The sumac species is a large shrub or small tree growing especially in sandy soils along roadsides, in grasslands and along forest edges. It is the only sumac native to all forty-eight contiguous states. The raw young sprouts were eaten by Native Americans as salad. The sour red fruit can be chewed to quench thirst or prepared as a drink similar to lemonade. The leaves were rolled and smoked to treat asthma. The bark, boiled in milk, is a treatment for burns.

Smooth sumac provides cover for rabbits, chipmunks, and other small animals including birds. Larger animals such as deer browse on its twigs and fruit year-round.

American Robin

Turdus migratorius

Dorothy: As a child the first bird I knew by name was a robin, and seeing my first robin of the spring has always brought a smile to my face. It seemed the most natural thing in the world that I would do a portrait of this bird.

Though spying a robin on the lawn seems to be a harbinger of spring, these song birds can be found year-round in most of the continental United States. The reason that we usually don't see them on lawns during the winter is that the ground is very cold or frozen and worms are difficult to wrench from the earth. In the winter, robins feed mostly on fruits and berries, including chokecherries, hawthorn, dogwood, sumac fruits, and juniper berries. One study suggested that robins may try to round out their diet by selectively eating fruits that have bugs in them. In spring and summer they eat large numbers of earthworms as well as insects and some snails. (They have rarely been recorded eating shrews, small snakes, and aquatic insects.)

Both the male and the female robin have similar plumage, although females have paler heads that contrast with the darker gray of their backs. In spring, males attract females by singing, raising and spreading their tails, shaking their wings, and inflating their white-striped throats.

An American robin can produce three successful broods in one year. On average, though, only 40 percent of nests successfully produce young. Only 25 percent of those fledglings survive to November. From that point on, about half of the robins alive in any year will make it to the next. Despite the fact that a lucky robin can live to be fourteen years old, the entire population turns over on average every six years.

Although many robins have succumbed to lead poisoning, viral infections, and many other hazards of urban life such as predatory cats, flying into windows, and so forth, robin populations as a whole (monitored across America for the past forty years) have slowly increased.

The American robin was named after the European robin because it has a red breast, but it is not closely related to that species. Actually, it's the largest member of the thrush family.

Quaking Aspen

Populus tremuloides

Heidi: Aspen trees are mostly recognized for their trunks and in the fall for their golden leaves fluttering in the breeze. They captured my attention because of the gracefully down-curved catkins, or flowering parts of the branch, while I sat under them one early spring.

This is a small to medium-size tree with a slender whitish to light green trunk marked with the characteristic dark "eyes." The leaves have pointed teeth along the margins and a long, flattened leafstalk that lets them flutter and rustle in the breeze.

Aspen stands can be found in diverse habitats such as mixed conifer forests, hardwood forests, or rocky, sandy, or clay soils.

Quaking aspen is the most widely distributed tree in North America. Most stems originate as root suckers that form extensive clones. One male clone in the Wasatch Range in Utah covers about 107 acres, has 47,000 trunks, and is often considered the world's most massive organism. Although the tree is symbolic of the Rocky Mountain region, its populations here have dropped sharply over the last century. This may be because of fire suppression practices, as aspen benefit when fires clear away conifers, giving the aspen the sunny open ground they need to send up shoots. Another hypothesis is that the drop is linked to the decline in wolf populations, as wolves keep elk, moose, and deer vigilant and on the move thus preventing them from settling in one place where they eat all of the aspen shoots.

Aspen have been used for medicine (tea from bark to treat skin problems, leaves to relieve pain and fever), food (the inner bark provided a sweet treat for some northern tribes; the bitter leaf buds and young catkins are edible and rich in vitamin C), tipi poles, paddles, sauna benches, playground equipment, pulp, and chopsticks.

Heidrun

Populus tremuloides

Yellow-rumped Warbler

Setophaga coronata (also classified as *Dendroica coronata*)

Heidi: Once I see these nimble flyers, flitting this way and that among the as yet leaf-less branches, I know spring is here.

This early spring migrant is a widespread wood warbler and has four distinct patches of yellow, particularly the yellow splash just above the point where the tail feathers begin. The Audubon's warbler with the yellow throat is more common in the West, and the myrtle warbler with the white throat more common in the East. These two varieties do sometimes mate where their boundaries overlap.

The yellow-rumped warbler feeds on insects, spiders, caterpillars, grasshoppers, seeds, wax myrtle, bayberries (and many other berries), or a bit of sap from sugar maple trees at sugaring time. It is very active, typically foraging in outer tree canopies at mid-height, and often traveling in large flocks.

This species is perhaps the most versatile of all warblers. They often flit, flycatcher-like, out from their perches in short loops to catch flying insects.

Audubon's Warbler, yellow-throated
Dendroica coronata auduboni

Myrtle Warbler, white-throated
Dendroica coronata coronata

House Finch

Haemorhous mexicanus

Dorothy: In all seasons, I've seen these little birds in nearly every park and open space in the area. I love the way they chatter to one another. They are regulars at my bird feeder so it was easy to get good pictures of them.

House finches are small-bodied finches with fairly large beaks. The males are rosy red around the face and upper breast with a streaky brown back, belly, and tail. The females look similar to the males minus the red. House finches are gregarious birds that collect at feeders or perch high in nearby trees. Their diet is exclusively seeds and plant parts, which is rare in the bird world. They also feed their nestlings only plant foods.

The birds were sold illegally in New York City as "Hollywood finches," a marketing ploy. To avoid prosecution under the Migratory Bird Act of 1918, vendors and owners released the birds. There are an estimated 267 million to 1.7 billion house finches across North America.

House finches nest in a variety of deciduous and coniferous trees as well as on cactus and rock ledges. They also nest in or on buildings, using sites like vents, ledges, street lamps, ivy, and hanging planters. Occasionally they use the abandoned nests of other birds. They usually migrate only short distances, if at all.

Golden Currant

Ribes aureum

Heidi: They grow along paths, they grow along the water, with bright yellow flowers in the spring and beautiful red leaves in the fall and are a great example of the beauty of everyday plants.

The golden currant is a shrub that belongs to the gooseberry family and is extensively planted because of its fragrant bright yellow flowers in spring, the pretty berries, and the attractive leaves that turn bright red in fall. The spicey fragrance is similar to that of clover or vanilla. The berries range from black to red in color and sometimes yellow, and are edible but very tart. The flowers are also edible. The leaves have three widely spreading lobes. Golden currant grows in plains and foothill sites from Alberta to Mexico.

The bush can reach ten feet in height, spreads by underground suckers, and is useful for erosion control. It provides cover for wildlife and if browsed it develops denser foliage. Native Americans mixed dried currants with dried, powdered bison meat to make pemmican. The twigs and leaves of the golden currant can be used for yellow, brown, gold, and olive-green dyes.

Golden currant with
      Arachne checkerspot

Ribes aureum with
      Poladryas arachne

Eurasian Collared Dove

Streptopelia decaocto

Heidi: For this bird I had to go no farther than my backyard where it gathers regularly around the bird feeder.

This dove has a telltale black narrow crescent collar around the neck and an overall sandy color. It is bigger than the mourning dove, but slimmer. In flight and when perched the

wingtips are darker than the rest of the wing. These doves perch on telephone poles, wires, and large trees and give incessant three-syllable coos. When walking, they bob their heads and flick their tails.

Males and females are virtually indistinguishable; juveniles differ in having a poorly developed collar. The doves are almost always seen in pairs and, like many birds, are loyal to their mates. The female lays two eggs in a stick nest, which she incubates during the night and the male incubates during the day. Three to four broods a year is common.

Introduced to the Bahama's in the 1970s, the Eurasian dove has since spread across much of the U.S. It is often found in urban areas and gardens, but also in the vicinity of farm buildings and grain silos. Its range is expected to expand farther.

White Ash

Fraxinus americana

Heidi: To stand beneath the brilliantly flaming foliage of a white ash is to have experienced the iridescent colors of otherworldly realms.

Ashes, the only members of the olive family with compound leaves, have opposite, pinnately compound leaves (pinnate leaves are multiply-divided arising from a common axis). Most ashes are deciduous. In most ashes the flowers are tiny (less than a quarter-inch wide) and wind-pollinated. Male and female flowers usually occur on separate trees and in most species are similar in color. The fruit is a one-sided green samara (a fruit with wing-like expansions) maturing to brown and occurring in hanging clusters.

White ash is a medium-size tree with a tall, straight trunk whose bark fissures form a diamond pattern. It has a dense, symmetrical crown and is planted as an ornamental for its spectacular autumn foliage. Its range extends from Texas to Ontario, and east to the Atlantic Ocean.

This tree is best known as "the tree that hits home runs." Baseball batters have long favored ash wood for its strength and springiness. However, this tradition may change. In the 1990s, an iridescent green beetle called the emerald ash borer came into this country from Asia and by some estimates this bug has already killed more than fifty million trees, and researchers are rushing to find ways to stop it.

Fraxinus americana
White Ash   Heidrun

Wild Rose

Rosa woodsii

Dorothy: To me the wild rose, with its delicate pink blossoms, is one of the most beautiful flowers of spring. But I like it even better in the fall when the leaves turn every color from gold to yellow and red to rust, with the bright red shiny hips that seem to glow.

America's native rose species are wild flowering shrubs that provide full spectrum pollen for bees, nesting places for birds, and seclusion for small mammals. Their fruits, called hips, are tasty treats for wildlife as well as a powerhouse of important antioxidants for humans. Native roses are important components of food forests and land restoration projects.

Along the Front Range, the wild rose blooms from June to July. The flowers are two to three inches in diameter. The bushes range in height from twenty-four to forty-eight inches. Its stems are covered with small cactus-like thorns. During late summer and early fall the rose produces red fruit that are claimed to be high in vitamin C.

There are over one hundred species of wild roses worldwide, some native to North America, many from the Orient and Europe. Unlike cultivated roses, which were bred to cover sexual organs with a confusion of extra petals, wild roses are all single with exactly five petals—never more—and almost all of them are pink, with a few whites and reds, and even fewer that range toward yellow.

Along the Front Range there are two truly wild species. *Rosa arkansana* and *Rosa woodsii*. These two species are very difficult to discern. The *Rosa arkansana* is said to have more thorns, but even the best botanists will quarrel about the identification of these two.

cm

Wild Rose   *Rosa woodsii*

Black-tailed Prairie Dog

Cynomys ludovicianus

Dorothy: Until we started this project, I had seen prairie dogs mostly by the side of the road as I drove by and, of course, as road-kill. I had never stopped to watch them. I was totally unaware of how playful and social they are. They spend so much time interacting with each other. They work hard at digging and repairing their burrows, but they also take time to play and groom each other. Now, after watching for just a short time, I can pick out family members and can observe their individual personalities. It seems to me that there are happy prairie dogs and crabby ones. Some want to play and joke around and others have a more serious got-to-work attitude. Now, prairie dog watching is one of my favorite things to do. To me, it beats reality TV for entertainment!

There are five different species of prairie dogs, but the most widespread is the black-tailed prairie dog, named for the little tip of black on its tail. All five species occupy separate ranges, with no part of their natural ranges overlapping.

Prairie dogs are not dogs, they are rodents like squirrels and chipmunks and marmots. Early pioneers crossing the Great Plains thought their calls sounded like the bark of a dog, and the name "prairie dog" was attached to them.

Black-tailed prairie dog colonies were once found across the Great Plains from southern Canada to northern Mexico. Their colonies probably once occupied 200 million acres within this 400-million-acre region, and were often tens of miles long. Today their small, scattered colonies occupy only 1-2 million acres. They were eradicated completely from Arizona.

Prairie dogs are considered a "keystone" species because their colonies create islands of habitats that benefit approximately 150 other species. They are also a food source for many animals, including coyotes, eagles, badgers, and critically endangered black-footed ferrets. Many species, like black-footed ferrets, tiger salamanders, and burrowing owls use their burrows as homes.

Prairie dogs help aerate and fertilize the soil, allowing a greater diversity of plants to thrive, but because they dig holes and tend to want to live in many places that people farm or ranch, they are considered pests and are still being eradicated.

Prairie dogs live in colonies in complex networks of underground tunnels that contain "rooms" for sleeping, rearing young, and storing food. They even have underground "bathrooms" where they eliminate their waste.

They are very social animals and live in close-knit family groups called "coteries" that usually consist of an adult male, one or two females, and their young offspring. These coteries are grouped together in neighborhoods called "wards." Then several wards together make a colony or town. Colonies are easily identified by the raised-burrow entrances that give the diminutive prairie dogs some extra height when acting as sentries and watching for signs of danger.

Prickly Poppy

Argemone Pleicantha

Dorothy: The prickly poppy has an absolutely stunning white flower, but the leaves and stems are so full of prickles that I have no desire to pick one! The next best thing was to do a portrait ... and that, I did. When I took the photograph of the flower, the fritillary had just flown from it so I included it as well.

This wildflower is in the same family as are the more common garden poppies. Along the Front Range they are found in sunny, dry, and sandy areas along roadsides and brushy hillsides. It is an annual plant that blooms in June and July. The blooms are long lasting, and each plant has multiple blooms. The flowers are pollinated by butterflies, bees, and beetles.

The spines and prickles protect the prickly poppy from most animals—and vice versa ... every part of the plant is poisonous if ingested.

Variegated Fritillary

Euptoieta claudia

The upperside of this butterfly is tawny orange with thick dark veins and markings and black spots near the margin. The hind wing margin is angled and slightly scalloped. The underside of the hind wing has a mottled pattern. The wingspan is about one and a half to three inches.

Eggs are laid singly on host plant stems and leaves and the caterpillars eat the leaves and flowers. They have about three broods from April to October. Caterpillar hosts include a variety of plants in several families including maypops, may apple, violets, purslane, stonecrop, and moonseed.

The adults eat nectar from several plant species including butterflyweed, common milkweed, dogbane, peppermint, red clover, swamp milkweed, and tickseed sunflower. Fritillaries are seen mostly in open sunny areas such as prairies, fields, pastures, road edges, and landfills.

Argemone pleicantha - Southwest Prickly Poppy

Euptoieta claudia - Variegated Fritillary

Red-tailed Hawk

Buteo jamaicensis

Heidi: I went for a walk with my small grandson one August when I saw this big bird up in an old cottonwood tree. Digging the camera out of the diaper bag, I tried to sneak closer—pretty much a joke given the raptor's vigilance and eyesight. Much to my surprise he did not fly off, but instead landed on the ground a mere four to five feet away from me. It looked like he had found a mole or small rodent in the tall grass and was beginning to devour it. I have seen red-tailed hawks many times after that, but never so close. My little grandson brought me luck.

This large raptor is probably the most common raptor in North America. It has a chestnut-colored tail, broad rounded wings, and a short wide tail. Large females might look like eagles from a distance. Red-tailed hawks boast a range of plumages tailored to the peculiarities of different regions. Western red-tails tend to be darker than eastern birds. In the West, some dark-phase (morph) red-tails are a solid dark brown except for the rusty tail. Another feature as distinctive as its red tail is the "bellyband"—the dark swath of feathers that runs across the bird's underparts. The bellyband is useful as a field mark and also provides the hawk some camouflage. Without one to break up the bird's outline, a perched red-tail would stand out like a beacon.

Red-tailed hawks are birds of open country and tend to soar in wide circles over open fields with heavy wing beats, flapping as little as possible to conserve energy. They attack in a slow, controlled dive, feet forward, unlike the falcon's steep dive. When soaring or flapping its wings, it typically travels around 40 mph, but when diving may exceed 120 mph. Because they are so common and easily trained as capable hunters, the majority of hawks captured for falconry in the U.S. are red-tails. They can be found perching on fence posts, telephone poles, or trees standing alone at the edge of a field. They eat mostly mammals and are therefore rarely seen at bird feeders, unlike the Cooper's hawk or the sharp-shinned hawk.

Red-tails reach sexual maturity at two to three years of age. It is monogamous, mating with the same individual for many years, only taking a new mate when its original mate dies. In the wild, red-tailed hawks have reach the age of twenty-five.

Heidrun   Red-tailed hawk

155

Mule Deer

Odocoileus hemionus

Heidi: Mule deer are everywhere—in the middle of the day, on a busy six-lane city highway, I collided with one.

Mule deer or black-tailed deer occur in the western half of the U.S., extending from the arctic south to Mexico. The males can weigh from 125 to 400 pounds and the females from 100 to 150 pounds, and both are largest in the Rocky Mountains. The largest recorded antler spread is 47.5 inches. Both male and female are reddish in the summer and bluish-gray in winter, usually with a whitish rump patch. The tail is either black or black-tipped and the ears are very large—hence the name. The antlers occur only on males and branch equally and are not prongs from a main beam.

Mule deer habitat includes coniferous forests, desert shrubs, chaparral, grass- land with shrubs, and in urban areas, golf courses, greenways, irrigation ditches, parks, and backyards.

Spotted young, or fawns, are born in the spring after an average gestation period of about seven months and are able to walk within minutes after their birth.

Besides humans, the three leading preda- tors of mule deer are coyotes, gray wolves, and cougars.

Rocky Mountain Bee Plant

Cleome serrulata

Heidi: I love weeds (with much less fervor in my garden, though) because they seem to defy the odds of their adverse surroundings. The same holds true for the Rocky Mountain bee plant. The delicate, but large pink flowers sit on long slender stems in the hottest, rockiest, driest places the Front Range can offer. Displaying their generous blossoms as late as August, they offer a welcome contrast to their otherwise parched surroundings and in the process attract all kinds of pollinators. Go bee plant!

The Rocky Mountain bee plant, or spider plant, is an annual herb, eight to sixty inches tall, with branches. It flowers from June to August and the fruits are dry, narrow, and spindle-shaped with egg-shaped seeds inside. It grows in rocky prairies and wastelands. It was already known to Octavius Horatius, a Roman physician of the fourth century, who used the name *Cleome* for a related plant. *Serrulata* means "little saw," referring to the saw-tooth leaf margins on some individual plants.

Surprisingly, this attractive but strong-smelling plant was used by some Native Americans as a food source. The leaves were cooked for greens like spinach, sometimes with corn, or were dried for winter usage. The seeds were ground for flour.

The Tewa tribe used this plant, which they called *guaco,* for paint. They boiled the plants until the liquid blackened. This thick fluid could be dried, and when soaked in water used as paint for their pottery decorations. The plant was important enough to the Tewa to be mentioned in songs.

There has even been archaeological evidence suggesting that *Cleome* was collected in quantity by prehistoric people of the Southwest, and that it may have been encouraged through tending, or even planted.

Rocky Mountain Bee Plant
Cleome serrulata

Crabapple

Malus sp.

Dorothy: In this painting of crabapple blossoms, I wanted to do something to bring to light the fact that our honeybees (who are the main pollinators of cultivated fruit trees) are in peril. Whole hives of them are dying at an alarming rate all over the world. To symbolize this plight, I made the bees in this illustration very difficult to find. There are ten bees hidden within the painting.

Crabapple blossoms appear in Colorado in April to May, depending on the variety, elevation, and weather conditions. There are many varieties of crabapples and the flowers vary from pink to white. The size and colors of the apple also vary. Crabapple trees are closely related to apple trees, which are also *Malus*, grown for fruit. The main difference is that the crabapple fruit is two inches in diameter or less; fruit greater than two inches is classified as an apple. The crabapple tree depends on insects (mostly bees) to pollinate the fruit.

Although many people think of the apple as American, it was actually imported from Europe sometime before 1600.

In the nineteenth century, apples came in all shapes and guises, some with rough, sand-papery skin, others as misshapen as potatoes, and ranging from the size of a cherry to bigger than a grapefruit. Colors ran the entire spectrum with a wonderful impressionistic array of patterning—flushes, stripes, splashes, and dots. There was an apple for every community, taste, purpose, and season, with winter varieties especially prized. Today, fewer than one hundred varieties are commercially cultivated, and of those, a mere handful is found in grocery stores.

Some apples are bred for their fruit, but the crabapple is now grown mostly as an ornamental tree. It is, however, a favorite of many species of birds as well as coyotes, foxes, raccoons, and skunks.

Blue Jay
Cyanocitta christata

Dorothy: They wake me in the morning with their loud chatter. They monopolize my bird feeder—they frighten the smaller birds away. I really can't explain why, but I love these little rascals! I really enjoyed painting this blue jay.

The blue jay is a large-crested bird with a broad rounded tail. They are in the Corvidae family, and are related to magpies and crows. Blue jays are smaller than crows but larger than robins. They are light gray on the breast and various shades of blue and black above. Males and females are almost identical, with the male being slightly larger.

Known to be "noisy," their calls reach long distances. They have been known to sound an alarm call when hawks or other dangers are near, and smaller birds often recognize this call and hide themselves away accordingly.

Blue jays are known for their intelligence and complex social systems with tight family bonds. Their fondness for acorns is credited with helping spread oak trees after the last glacial period.

They have been known to eat the eggs and nestlings of smaller birds, and it is this practice that has tarnished their reputation with many bird lovers, although this may not be as common as once typically thought. The fact is, they eat mostly acorns, nuts and seeds, small insects and caterpillars.

Common for centuries in eastern and central North America, blue jays have gradually extended their range to eastern Colorado. They are fairly social and are typically found in pairs, family groups, and flocks. Their migration is a bit of a mystery to scientists. Large flocks have been known to migrate south for the winter, but some individual birds may winter in all parts of their range. One year individual birds may migrate and then not the next year. Likely it is weather related and how abundant the winter food sources are. They have been seen in backyards and parks along the Front Range in all seasons of the year.

Cooper's Hawk
Accipiter cooperii

Heidi: One May morning I went around a bend on my walk and stopped dead in my tracks because a few feet ahead of me, on a big branch hanging over the path, sat a big hawk in full plumage, preening itself. I immediately grabbed my camera and just started shooting without even properly focusing before he finally flew off. Other passersby told me about his nest close by, which I then looked for and found. At that point I didn't know what I had seen, and after some research I learned that it was a Cooper's hawk. Later that year and the following year I saw him in action flying between the trees or coming back from the hunt with slow glides, barely missing me as I crouched in the shrubbery under trees feeling the "swoosh" of his wingbeats—an exhilarating sensation!

Also known as "chicken hawk," this medium-size hawk has a blue-gray back and a somewhat darker head. The underparts are pale and the chest and belly have orange-reddish horizontal striping, which is brown in juveniles. The eyes in adults are bright red, but yellow in juveniles. The Cooper's hawk has a classic accipiter shape with broad rounded wings and a long rounded tail.

This rather common hawk is among the world's most skillful fliers as it tears through cluttered tree canopies in pursuit of prey, which is almost exclusively small to mid-size birds. They have been known to rob nests and may supplement their diet with small mammals such as chipmunks, hares, mice, squirrels, and bats. As woodland birds, Cooper's hawks are most likely to prowl the woods' edge with just a few wing beats followed by a glide. They are extremely similar to their smaller look-alikes, the sharp-shinned hawk, and therefore difficult to identify. Both species are sometimes unwanted guests at bird feeders looking for an easy meal.

Cooper's hawks are monogamous, but most do not mate for life. They have been known to live as long as twelve years in the wild. The hawk lives in Colorado year-round, but sightings have been primarily in summer.

Cooper's Hawk
Accipiter cooperii

Scot's Pine

Pinus sylvestris

Dorothy: I like pine cones. I have a collection of them from nearly every cone-bearing tree in Colorado. In this painting I wanted to show both the male and female cones, and the mature second-year cone that was still clinging to the branch.

Scot's pine, sometimes called scotch pine, is a fast-growing evergreen tree, growing up to sixty feet tall with a spread of twenty-five to thirty feet at maturity. It is pyramidal in shape when it is young, and it becomes more round-topped and irregular as it ages. The tree was first introduced from Europe in the 1700s and has become naturalized in eastern North America. It grows quite well in Colorado as well. You can see examples of both young and mature trees in most parks in the Denver area.

The needles occur in bunches of two, usually twisted, are two to four inches long, and are light green in color. Young twigs are green, turning brown with age, and they stay on the tree for about three years.

The cones are from one and a half inches to three inches long, gray to brown, and usually falling at maturity.

The bark is one of the tree's best features. It is orange, thin, and smooth on the upper trunk, often peeling in papery flakes with maturity. The lower trunk tends toward orangeish-brown to gray, becoming fissured into longitudinal plats with maturity. The open branching habit of the tree shows off the attractive bark all year long. Young Scot's pine are commonly used as Christmas trees.

Pinus sylvestris

Scots Pine

Swainson's Hawk

Buteo swainsoni

Heidi: Perched on trees, perched on fence posts—this raptor captured my attention because of its cool, understated elegance. To focus on just that, I deliberately selected a barely-there back-ground—let all the attention be on this beautiful raptor.

The elegant Swainson's hawk belongs to the Buteo family. Buteos are large, thickset hawks with broad wings and wide, rounded tails. Buteos tend to soar high in wide circles. There is much variation among this species, but the females are always larger than the males (which is called dimorphism). Most Swainson's hawks are light-bellied birds with a dark or reddish-brown chest and brown or gray upper parts; females tend to have brown heads. Young birds are usually streaked below.

Proportioned much like the red-tailed hawk, but with wings more pointed, it hunts rodents in flight with wings held in a shallow V. Sometimes it even runs after insects on the ground. It nests in the western United States and Canada and winters in South America and thus is among the world's long-distance champions, with a migration of up to 14,000 miles, lasting at least two months.

The oldest wild Swainson's hawk on record is twenty-four years.

Swainson's hawk
Buteo swainsoni

Common Raven

Corvus corax

Dorothy: When I saw this old iron gate at a local park, I had an immediate picture in my mind of a raven perched on it as if to guard the entrance. I stalked ravens for about a year before I got pictures good enough to use as photo references. The light had to be just right to get highlights on those blue-black feathers! Finally, my vision was realized!

Ravens are among the most intelligent of all birds. They have a reputation for solving complicated problems. This makes them effective predators. They sometimes work in pairs to raid nests of other birds, with one bird distracting an incubating adult and the other waiting to grab an egg or chick as soon as it's uncovered. They've been seen waiting in trees as ewes give birth, then attacking the newborn lambs.

Common ravens can mimic the calls of other bird species. When raised in captivity, they can even imitate human words. One rather famous raven, raised from birth in captivity, was taught to mimic the word "nevermore." If a member of a mated pair is lost, its mate reproduces the calls of its lost partner to encourage its return. Ravens have been observed calling wolves to the site of dead animals. The wolves open the carcass, leaving the scraps more accessible to the birds.

In the field, ravens and crows can be tough to distinguish. In flight, the end of a raven's tail is diamond shaped while the end of the crow's tail is flat. In voice, ravens tend to be croaky and raspy while the crows generally call a clear "caw, caw, caw." Ravens have a larger body and more robust bill. Sometimes just a look at the face and more ruffled feathers around the bill will give you a good sense of the larger size of the raven.

Owing to its size, gregariousness, and its defensive abilities, the common raven has few natural predators.

Lifespans in the wild are typically ten to fifteen years. In captive or protected conditions, they have lived for more than forty years.

Juvenile ravens are among the most playful of bird species. They have been observed sliding down snowbanks, apparently purely for fun. They are also one of only a few wild animals that make their own toys—they have been observed breaking off twigs to play with socially.

Bibliography

Balmer, Elizabeth. *Pocket Guide to Butterflies and Moths.* Parragon Publishing, 2007.

Barker, Joan. *Field Guide to the Flowers of North America.* Parragon Publishing, 2006.

Book of North American Birds. Reader's Digest, 1990.

Carter, Jack and Martha. *Common Southwestern Native Plants.* Mimbres Publishing, 2009.

Colorado Division of Parks and Wildlife magazine articles.

Evans, Arthur. *Field Guide to Insects and Spiders of North America.* Sterling Publishing, 2008.

Johnson, J. and Gary Larson. *Grassland Plants of S. Dakota and the Northern Great Plains.* South Dakota State University, 2007.

Kershaw, Linda. *Edible Medicinal Plants of the Rockies.* Lone Pine Publishing, 2000.

Kershner, Mathews, Nelson, and Spellenberg. *Field Guide to Trees of North America.* Sterling Publishing, 2008.

Kindscher, Kelly. *Edible Wild Plants of the Prairie.* University Press of Kansas, 1987.

Liguori, Jerry. *Hawks at a Distance.* Princeton University Press, 2011.

National Audubon Society. *Field Guide to Wildflowers, Western Region.* A. Knopf, Chanticleer Press, 2001.

National Audubon Society. *Field Guide to Trees, Western Region.* A. Knopf, Chanticleer Press, 1980.

Paulson, Dennis. *Dragonflies and Damselflies of the West.* Princeton University Press, 2009.

Sterry, P. and B. Small. *Birds of Western North America.* Princeton University Press, 2009.

Stokes, Donald and Lillian. *Stokes Field Guide to Birds of North America*, Little, Brown and Company, 2010.

Taylor, Ronald. *Sagebrush Country.* Mountain Press Publishing, 1992.

Whitson, Burrill, Dewey, Cudney, Nelson, Lee, and Parker. *Weeds of the West.* Western Society of Weed Science, 2012.

On-line Resources

Colorado State University Extension, CMG Garden Notes, http://www.ext.colostate.edu

Cornell Lab of Ornithology, www.allaboutbirds.org

National Geographic, www.animals.nationalgeographic.com

Trees of North America, www.treesofnorthamerica.net

USDA National Agriculture Library, www.invasivespeciesinfo.gov

USDA Natural Resources Conservation Service, http://plants.usda.gov

U.S. Department of Agriculture, NRCS Plant Guide, www.ncrs.usa.gov

Washington Department of Fish and Wildlife, http://wdfw.wa.gov

Wikipedia, http://wikipedia.org